zen

and the art of

cooking

zen

and the art of

cooking

jon sandifer

SOURCEBOOKS, INC.®
NAPERVILLE, ILLINOIS

contents

what i

All of us can relate to occasions in our lives when we have felt completely at one with ourselves and the world. These moments of clarity and inner peace frequently occur when we have no distractions and when we are in nature. Whether it is watching a sunset, walking along a beach, sitting by a mill pond, these moments can be described as Zen experiences. Sometimes these glimpses of truth and harmony occur while we are involved in some form of daily activity. Even while caught up in the act of "doing"—operating at an almost mechanical level—our mind can open to new possibilities.

For me, Zen is a journey and not a religion. For many, it can be a way of life that involves living simply, letting go of the past, and releasing oneself from material and emotional attachments in order to receive new insights. Through Zen we can find and experience satori—the Ultimate Truth. However, the journey towards this goal involves first working with the Relative Truth. The path to the Relative Truth can involve the practice of Zen meditation, cooking, archery, flower arranging, writing poetry, martial arts, fasting, or numerous other pastimes.

s zen?

Taking on an additional recreational pursuit to help us relax and rejuvenate may have the opposite effect from what we intended—just trying to find enough time to do it can be stressful. And few of us would go so far as to abandon our jobs and families to join a Zen monastery. Yet meditation does not have to be an intense and isolating act conducted in a motionless state. Instead, think about taking a part of your daily routine and turning it into an opportunity to meditate. For example, if you prepare at least one meal a day, why not make the time cooking into the focus for your Zen practice and experience each part of it as a rewarding journey? By turning the relatively mundane activities of selecting, preparing, and eating food into an opportunity for self-reflection, you do not have to set aside more of your valuable time to find quiet moments of peace. Spending just twenty or thirty minutes daily preparing food can make all the difference in replenishing our spirit. The Japanese art of *shojin ryori* ("food to develop spirituality") provides a profound working model of how cooking and spiritual practices can be interwoven. This discipline forms the basis of Japanese temple cooking and is practiced to this day.

the four noble truths

The essence of Zen can be discovered by reflecting on the four Noble Truths. They act as a reminder of the journey and can be interpreted and practiced in different ways. These Noble Truths can be related to the subject of this book: food and cooking.

❶ we are all suffering

The first step to understanding the four Noble Truths is to recognize that we are all a product of the experiences we have undergone in our upbringing, our education, and the dominant lifestyle of our society. Our potential as human beings is limited by having to live within the constraints of these experiences, which collectively can be called our conditioning, as well as the more natural constraints imposed by our humanity.

With regard to food and cooking, we need to recognize the conditioning in the way we were taught to cook, our attitudes toward mass-produced foods, and the seductive powers of advertising which impact what we eat and how we prepare it.

❷ letting go of attachments

The second Noble Truth involves a deep process of self-reflection in which we take an inventory of our emotional and material attachments. In cooking, this involves questioning our attitude towards food and our relationship with it. Do we, for example, eat to cheer ourselves up? Do we choose food products that remind us of our childhood to achieve a sense of contentment?

❸ realizing there is another way

For many, the third Noble Truth means hitting a wall, for others a deep intuitive insight bubbles to the surface and points them in another direction. In relation to cooking, it involves re-addressing how we cook, and what we cook.

❹ the eight fold path

The Eight Fold Path is the fourth of the Noble Truths. It is important to remember that in Zen there are no rules, there is no dogma—you are ultimately your own teacher and guide. If we take the clues that Zen masters have delivered throughout the centuries and apply them to our relationship with food and cooking, then cooking itself can become a form of meditation. The Eight Fold Path consists of the following points, some of which concern ethical conduct (right speech, action, and livelihood), others concern mental discipline (right effort, attention, and concentration), while others are facets of wisdom (right thought and understanding). In Zen, it is possible to begin at any point along the Path, since all parts interact.

1 right speech avoids lying, and does not encourage malice or hatred. Avoid cooking and eating when you are angry or resentful and likely to curse your implements. Express yourself with appreciation and grace.

2 right action avoids taking what is not given and uses well what is yours. It involves the selection and preparation of the right foods and setting up the kitchen using the principles of Feng Shui to give maximum support to the cook.

3 right livelihood means earning a living in a way that does not cause harm to others. It also implies that we must eat in balance with our way of life and our jobs. Do not, for instance, eat large amounts of stamina-producing food to do a sedentary job.

4 right effort stimulates good thoughts and avoids extremes. It achieves its purpose with the least resistance and effort.

5 right attention applies to activities of the mind and body. Give your full attention to the preparation of the meal. It shows your discipline and commitment to seeing the process through.

6 right concentration trains the mind through meditation and must be used in digesting the moment. All the love and care taken in producing a meal may be lost without concentrating on and enjoying what you are eating.

7 right understanding sees the world as it really is, without delusions. Whichever way we choose to take along the road of Relative Truth, we need to keep what we learn in perspective, so that we are able to tap into the great well of wisdom without wasting it through poor judgement.

8 right thought purifies the mind and heart. Getting ourselves into the right state of "being" rather than "doing" is essential in the Zen approach to cooking.

evolution and food

One of the first steps to take in letting go of our cravings, our conditioning, and attachments is to compare what we eat today with how our ancestors ate. What foods have developed in step with the evolution of human beings? To analyze this involves going beyond our modern understanding of a "normal" diet.

As human beings, we have the extraordinary capacity to digest almost any food available. In one sense we are not dissimilar to rats, and it is interesting to note how many scientific experiments have been carried out on these rodents to determine what might benefit or harm humans. Our digestive system itself is a good indicator of what we are capable of absorbing. Unlike a carnivore, which has a short digestive system allowing flesh to pass through it quickly, or a herbivore, which has a long digestive tract to allow maximum absorption, we omnivores come somewhere in the middle.

Our teeth also give an indication of what we are capable of digesting. We have 32 teeth, of which 20 are premolars and molars, designed for grinding primitive grass seeds, grains, and nuts. We have eight incisors, which are perfect for breaking down vegetables, and only four canine teeth for tearing into animal food or fish. Overall, this is an indication that our diet requires an intake of at least 40 percent cereal products; some 30 percent vegetables, salad, and fruit; and a much smaller proportion of flesh. Naturally, this can be adapted according to the climate in which we live, our activities, and our own special requirements.

Once human beings discovered fire and learned to cook, our culture expanded rapidly through agriculture and the building of communities. Research shows that the oldest ingredients among modern foods are grains and legumes. Even now, in the third millennium, some 75 percent of the world's population still base their daily diet on grain products.

Whatever culture you choose to look at around the world you will find it has the following four points in common with all others:

• The predominance of cereal grains and legumes. • Soup or stew production. • Vegetables are eaten on a daily basis. • Fermented foods are eaten on a daily basis.

The modern trend in the industrialized world has been a shift away from this diet. At the same time there has been a rise in degenerative disease, with almost epidemic levels of heart disease, cancer, and nervous disorders. We cannot ignore the very real possibility that what we eat in our youth affects our susceptibility to degenerative disease in later life. Western diets include the following four categories:

1 A predominance of food derived from animals, including meat, dairy products, eggs, and even fish.

2 Cereal grain replaced by the tuber–or potato–which is not a cereal grain, nor a vegetable, but actually part of the nightshade family.

3 Cereal grains largely replaced by refined carbohydrates–including white flour products, sugar, and highly processed foods.

4 Only small amounts of fresh fruit and vegetables.

When it comes to selecting your foods, try to keep the evolutionary process in mind. In determining which ingredients to use, experiment by using a higher proportion of grains and legumes, make sure that you include soup every day, eat plenty of fresh vegetables, and include some form of fermented food to aid digestion.

food for the soul

The well-worn adage that "we are what we eat" does hold true. We must realize that what we are eating or have eaten recently has a direct bearing on how we are being, our chi, and our consciousness.

The source and creator of all our food is the environment which provides the ingredients of soil, water, and air. As we cook and digest this food, it becomes our blood. Half of our blood is made up of plasma, which regenerates itself every ten days. It is easy to understand why if we make a conscious change in our diet over a period of ten days that it will affect how we feel and perceive the world around us. This blood in turn nourishes and regenerates our internal organs—the heart, lungs, pancreas, kidneys, spleen, and liver. The health of these organs in turn brings vitality, awareness and acuity to our nervous system. Made up not only of our brain and its cells, and our spine and each individual nerve, the nervous system is paralleled with a charge of chi. In the Orient, this is known as our spiritual channel, and it has various connecting centers known as chakras where chi is focused and then distributed. This nervous system fuels our perception and our responses, which we call our consciousness.

the zen approach to cooking

The fundamental aim
of a Zen approach to cooking is
to open up this awareness in ourselves,
a process that can be enhanced by choosing
ingredients that match our evolution and support
our individual needs. I warmly invite you to share
my ideas and insights in this book. It is no ordinary
cook book. You will not find lists of 'shoulds' and
'should nots,' nor dense scientific explanations or
long lists of weights and measures in recipes.
The book is intended as a guide to the spirit
of cooking and our relationship with
food. Enjoy–and chew very,
very well.

chapter 1

feng shui: harmony in design

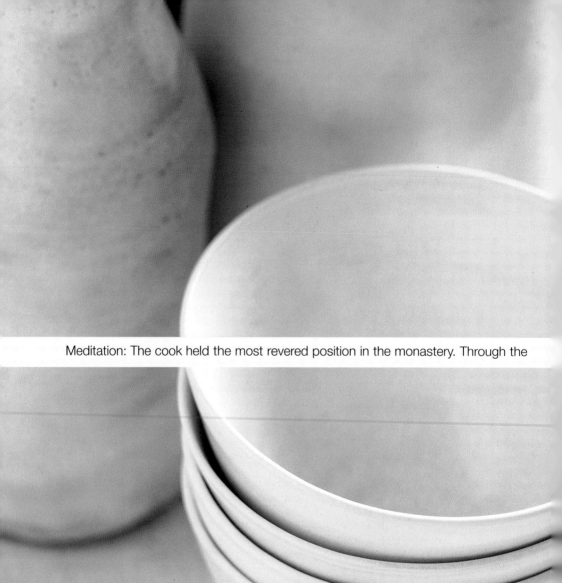

Meditation: The cook held the most revered position in the monastery. Through the clarity of his thinking and action he set the mood of all the monks in the monastery.

Foreigners in nineteenth-century China would ask what Feng Shui (pronounced Fung Shoy) was, only to be told that it means "wind and water–so-called because it is like wind, which you cannot comprehend, and like water, which you cannot grasp." It literally does mean wind and water, but in practical terms Feng Shui is the ancient Chinese art of placement which evolved during the Sung dynasty in China (c. A.D. 1100-1200). Its purpose is to create harmony, health, and prosperity for the inhabitants of the household. Although the subject itself can be taken through many layers of interpretation, I will explain the basic principles and show you how to apply them to your kitchen space and your dining area to help set the tone for cooking and eating.

in the kitchen

"Let us train our minds to desire what the situation demands"—Seneca

chi

If we think of our home in terms of how our body functions, then chí, or "cosmic breath" as the Chinese call it, is the equivalent of oxygen circulating in our lungs and blood. This vital force in all living beings has the potential to become highly charged, stagnant, or even disruptive. The whole purpose of Chinese medicine is to restore harmony to the chi of the body. By using acupuncture and herbs it is possible to keep the body in balance, thus preventing the onset of serious disease. Taking this principle—that prevention is better than cure—what are the issues to be aware of regarding the circulation of chi within the kitchen? There are three points to consider: how to avoid negative sources of chi, known as cutting chi; how to protect the chi; and how to enhance the chi.

cutting chi

One of the main differences between the modern structures of the kitchen and the natural landscape is the angular structure of appliances, shelves, cupboards, and doorways. Rivers are never completely straight, rocks are seldom angular, and hills and mountains are not box-shaped. Chi energy has a tendency to deflect itself off sharp edges and corners, and it has greater intensity after the deflection. For example, the edge of a shelf positioned close to your head while you are cooking will direct cutting chi toward you from the right angle the shelf makes with the wall. The outcome can be a feeling of pressure, antagonism, or even a headache.

The sources of this cutting chi within the kitchen

are worth noting and it is wise to position yourself away from them when cooking. The edges of counters and worktops, if they are aimed toward you while you are cooking, are common ones. Extractor fans above the stove are potentially troublesome—in many kitchens the edges are almost at forehead level.

The simplest solution to cutting chi is to round off the sharp edges. If that is not practical, you could position a plant with trailing leaves at the corner to obscure the edge. A tablecloth over a sharp-edged kitchen table can help, and covering bookshelves with some kind of drape or curtain will also work. As far as the extractor-fan hood is concerned, position it higher, if you can, to prevent the cutting chi from being directed at you.

protecting chi

Like a natural body of water, chi likes to circulate freely. The main source of chi in the home enters through the main door and windows of the property. Traditionally, the more animated (yang) activities of the home take place in rooms situated close to the front door, such as family rooms, meeting rooms, and even the dining area. Quieter (yin) activities, such as cooking and sleeping, should be located away from the front door to be protected from any torrent of chi. The ideal situation for the kitchen is to be on the ground floor, as far away as possible from the front door, and not visible from it. The stove should also never be visible from the front door.

When we are cooking, we intuitively need to feel comfortable and protected. On a subliminal level we would all feel uncomfortable if we were to cook with our back facing the entrance to the kitchen. Have you ever noticed that even when you are traveling on a train or sitting in a restaurant you like to see the entrance? In your kitchen, if it is impractical for you to see the door due to the position of your stove, try placing a mirror on the counter next to the stove and angle it in such a way that you can see the door. It is similar to having a driving mirror in a car to observe what is behind you.

Cooking in a "draught chi" is another situation to avoid. Avoid positioning yourself in a direct line between the entrance to the kitchen and any window or back door. Chi energy will enter the kitchen through the opening and most of this chi will then exit the room fairly swiftly in a direct line. Standing in this "draught" is distracting and has a tendency to allow your concentration or meditation to go out the window. If, due to the position of your stove, you are unable to stand in any other place, you can reduce the chi by placing a metal wind chime made up of five hollow tubes somewhere on the ceiling in a direct line between the door and whatever opening it faces. This will slow down and disperse fast moving chi.

Skylights, especially above the stove, act as a "chimney" for chi, which simply spirals up and disperses through the skylight. If you cannot change the design, you could place a metal wind chime at the highest point on the skylight to disperse and decelerate the loss of chi.

enhancing chi

Cooking is essentially a form of alchemy. The true source of this transmutation process begins with the element Fire. This element is obviously found in the source of heat—the stove—but is also reflected spiritually in terms of enlightenment, clarity, and vision. In Chinese medicine, the element that supports Fire is Wood. Wood is a literal translation and perhaps a better description is tree or plant life. In general, fixtures and fittings made of unfashioned wood within the kitchen are the best, together with colors that represent the element Tree, such as different shades of green for walls or tiling. It would be unwise to use too many blues, especially

dark blues and the color black, which are associated with Water, the element that suppresses Fire. Images and artwork provide us with subconscious reminders and messages wherever they are placed. Within the kitchen, uplifting images of plants and food are perfect. Lighting is a vital ingredient as this also represents the element Fire, and should be neither too bright nor too dim. The worst type of lighting is fluorescent. Working underneath the harshness of this source of Fire, together with the highly charged use of alternating current above your head, is very distracting. Ceiling spotlights aimed at your preparation area and stove are ideal.

"Act without
work

doing;
without effort."

Tao te Ching

water
wood
fire
earth
metal

There are five elements in traditional Chinese medicine. Before you arrange your kitchen, it is worth considering what these elements are and how they support or conflict with each other.

The element Water fuels and nurtures Wood, which in turn is the fuel of—and the creator of—Fire. As Fire dies down within this cycle it supports the element Earth which represents soil, ashes, and the soft condensing of material. With time and pressure, Earth creates Metal, which is associated with minerals and rocks. These ultimately disintegrate and liquefy, bringing the cycle back to Water.

There is also a cycle of potential conflicts among the five elements. Water can extinguish Fire; Fire can melt Metal; Metal cuts Wood; Wood, as trees and plants, can break up Earth through the roots; and Earth can dam the progress of Water, or absorb it.

In the kitchen the two elements that you need to be concerned about from a Feng Shui perspective are Fire and Water. Fire is obviously the stove, whereas Water can represent not only the sink but also the refrigerator, the freezer, and even a washing machine or dishwasher. To position these two elements adjacent to or opposite each other causes an imbalance of the chi within the space.

The solution is to introduce Wood as an intermediary element. If it is not practical to move the stove or the sink, then position something in between them that represents Wood–a painting of plants, trees, or shrubs; a wooden ornament; tiling that has plenty of green and images of plants; or an actual plant or a bunch of flowers.

The focal point of the kitchen is its source of heat—the stove. It is worth reflecting what source of "flame" you use. I personally favor the use of a real flame and would opt for a gas stove instead of an electric one any day. A flame is simply a microcosm of the sun—the source of our sustenance. A controllable gas flame is the closest we can get on a practical level to this source. While electric ovens and microwaves may not technically change the flavor of the food, they lack the chi charge of food cooked on a real flame.

It is important to remember that throughout civilization we have used a flame to cook our ingredients from the outside toward the inside. With a microwave stove, we throw this evolutionary trend into reverse. The process of microwave cooking, which acts through molecular friction to generate heat, begins at the center of the food and

the stove

works toward the outside.

Comparing gas with electric stoves is analogous to attending a concert or listening to it on the radio. While the sound of the music vibrating on your eardrums is much the same, is the experience the same? There is no real comparison between a live performance–the real thing–and a recording.

If you have always cooked with electricity, then provided you use good ventilation, it is worth experimenting for one month with gas cooking by using a twin-burner camping gas outfit. These are available from most camping stores. Before using it make sure that the unit is securely clamped to a countertop, that it has a regulator, and that the gas tubing meets safety standards. Installing a whole new gas stove is an expensive operation, but at least you can experience cooking with a real flame.

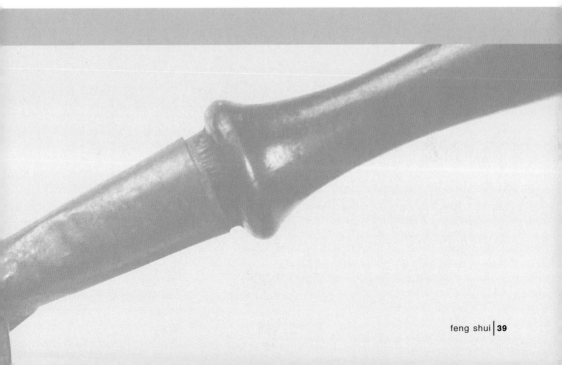

spring clean

Zen cooking is a truly creative art, and there is nothing worse than having to create magic in a kitchen that is not functional, clean, bright and airy. Like any artist, it is inspiring to begin with a clean canvas. Making a fresh start with this new approach to cooking can be helped profoundly if you keep the space simple, orderly, bright, and clean. To maximize the potential of allowing fresh chi to circulate in the kitchen and all its recesses means taking a long hard look at the space.

Begin by making sure that your windows are sparkling clean allowing fresh chi to enter the space for you to be inspired. In essence, chi has two qualities. It can be bubbly, fresh, alive, and healthy, which the Chinese call Sheng, or it can be stagnant, heavy, dark, clammy, or stuck, which the Chinese call Sha chi. The nearest natural elements to chi that we can perceive are undoubtedly wind and water. Noticing how air can stagnate in unventilated spaces, or how water can become a creek or an isolated pond, will give you an idea of what to look for. Stagnant chi in the kitchen is undoubtedly found in corners since chi moves in spirals and cannot circulate freely into the deep recesses of a right-angled corner. Get rid of all the cobwebs, dust, and oily patches where the ceiling meets the walls, where two walls join, in the backs of cupboards, behind and beside the stove, behind the refrigerator, and even behind the door if it is used infrequently.

At the same time have a good look in those cupboards. Old cans and jars of food that are well past their sell-by date or ingredients that you seldom use are simply adding to the clutter and attracting stagnant chi to them. Have a good look in the fridge as well, as this is a favorite hide-out for cold, damp, and stagnant chi.

Wearing your chi detective hat, take an objective look in the dreaded cupboard under the sink. It is surprising what you will find in there. Given that the kitchen is the source of our food, our blood, and our creativity, why do so many destructive elements lurk in the cupboard under the sink? You will probably find slug pellets, fly spray, ant powder, heavy duty bleaches, corrosive chemicals, as well as all manner of cobwebs, and even the trash can! Be ruthless in your clean out and designate all the "killers" to the trashcan or the garden shed or the garage, but please do not leave them in your kitchen!

the dining room

"Laughter is the shortest distance between two people"—Victor Borge

harmonious dining

Ultimately, common sense, practicality, and the use of Feng Shui principles can help to create an eating environment that is both comfortable and relaxing. It is fairly easy to generate an atmosphere of harmony, allowing individuals to converse freely, or if you dine alone, to feel comfortable with yourself.

In many ways, fast-food restaurants have taken these principles and turned them upside down to produce an atmosphere where customers will be initially attracted, eat quickly, and then leave without lingering over coffee. This is achieved by using bright lights, inviting colors, simple, stark, utility furniture that does not encourage you to stay, and finally the hovering presence of a cleaner or waiter. Another key to why fast-food restaurants have a turnover of clients is that their windows often fill entire sides of the building. This encourages chi to be at its most yang (active phase), unlike a domestic dining room or a quiet Italian restaurant where you can linger and enjoy your meal.

Eating is regarded as a private affair, and any room used for dining within the home is best situated further away from the busy, front part of the home. Being able to see the kitchen or the dining room from the front door will also encourage the occupants of the home to think continually about food and cooking, or at least be aware of it, and this can result in over-eating or constant snacking.

Leave the door of the dining room open when it is not in use to allow chi energy to circulate freely and to avoid the build up of stagnant chi. Whether we dine alone or with family or friends, the focus of our attention should always be around the table. In view of this it is unwise to have massive windows in the dining area which can take the focus of conversation and chi out of the room. If your home is located on a busy thoroughfare even a small window can cause a distraction. In either case, it is useful to have lightweight blinds or curtains to minimize the distractions.

furnishing the dining room

As we have already seen with Feng Shui applied in the kitchen, the first step in arranging a room is always to take care of any negative sources of chi, in particular cutting chi. Avoid chi energy being directed in a negative fashion from the sharp edges of furniture, the undersides of ceiling beams, or from angular structures outside that may direct cutting chi through the window into the room.

As far as overhead beams are concerned, the worst design would be one that "divided" the dining table into separate halves. Immediately this causes social division at the table and family arguments can ensue with one side disagreeing with the other. Remember also to avoid placing a dining room chair under an overhead beam. Sharp edges of cupboards or shelves can be softened by moving the piece of furniture so that the corner is not aimed at any chair; draping soft furnishings such as a table cloth or a mat over the corner; or positioning a plant that will trail over the edge and "hide" the sharp angle.

It is quite a common feature of a dining room to incorporate a central, overhanging lamp above the table. There is no problem with this, provided that the base of the overhanging lamp as it projects downward is either round, semicircular, or flat. Avoid any lamp that has a sharp protuberance at the base and ends in a point aimed at the center of the table. This is the ultimate in cutting chi—like shooting an arrow into the center of the table—and it can be the cause of disharmony and argument.

As a general rule, make sure that none of the chairs in the dining area have their backs to a door. Subliminally the person sitting in the chair will feel uneasy and concerned about who or what is about to come through the door behind them—not a situation in which to fully relax and enjoy a meal.

The décor of a dining room will certainly set the tone for conversations, relationships, and harmony. Yellow encourages conversation; green produce new ideas and has a calming effect; a splash of red brings laughter and inspiration; but blue, or at least a dominance of blue, is too cold. Artwork on the walls is best kept to a minimum to prevent the focus of conversation or eating from moving away from the table. A common Feng Shui feature, found not only in family homes in Asia but also in many restaurants, is a large mirror on the wall. This has the effect of doubling the size of the table and the food being served, and in turn creates an atmosphere of abundance, success, and generosity.

the dining table

The central feature of the dining room obviously needs to be the table itself. From the perspective of the Form School of Feng Shui, a table needs to be absolutely stable. Also, make sure that there are no sharp edges, and if the table is in sections, cover it with a cloth to give the impression of wholeness. Round tables are highly favored as they allow conversation and chi to circulate freely without any sense of hierarchy at the table. Square and octagonal tables are good as each individual has his or her space. Oval and rectangular tables create a dominating effect as the two individuals at the heads of the table are in a position of power or authority.

It is a good idea to have some form of central feature on the table which could include flowers, a plant, or a pair of candles. Try to avoid any feature that is too high and creates a wall or a barrier between you and the person opposite.

Dining room chairs and their design can also be drawn from aspects of the Form School of Feng Shui. Ideally they need to have a high back which is solid—even if it is cushioned—and reaches at least to shoulder level. Avoid chairs with arms as these create division between you and your neighbor, which, in turn, prevents chi from circulating smoothly around the table.

other dining areas

The size of your home or apartment may restrict you to having to eat in either the kitchen or the living room. The main consideration here, as with a dedicated dining room, is that the table is positioned out of the main thoroghfare. Avoid placing the table in a line between the door and a window or worse still the back door and the door of the kitchen. In both of these situations the dining table would be sitting in a draught of chi that flows between the two openings. Cooking and eating are two very different activities from a yin/yang perspective. While cooking we are in control of fire and time, and we need to have more presence and concentration, which are yang attributes. Eating, assimilating, reflecting, relaxing, or enjoying conversation are all yin attributes. If at all possible, try somehow to demarcate the relaxing zone, where you eat, from the busy area, where you prepare food and cook. This can be achieved by having, for example, different flooring for the two areas. The kitchen area could be tiled or stone-floored, whereas the dining area laid with wood or carpet. The actual cooking and preparation area needs to have fairly bright lights, whereas in the dining area lower, softer, more yin, lighting is better. If your dining table is situated in your living room or kitchen it can become a handy area to leave your papers, correspondence, magazines, telephone, or briefcase. Like the main table in a dining room, keep this table clear and focused on its real purpose—a space for you to eat, relax, and reflect.

breakfast bars

These are a Feng Shui nightmare! Usually the surface area for eating on is tight and narrow, and frequently there are overhanging shelves or wall units close to your head. Many breakfast bars face a wall, which is hardly the most exciting way to start a new day filled with infinite possibilities. In addition to these factors, they are usually positioned high off the floor which in itself creates a feeling of separation and aloofness. Finally, most people find themselves perched precariously on a tall stool with no back and therefore no support behind them. It all adds up to creating an atmosphere of speed, instability, and isolation.

In my work as a Feng Shui consultant, I have noticed that the major issues in people's lives who make use of some form of breakfast bar are poor communication and family disharmony. On closer questioning, I discover that at breakfast the family eats in a hurry and rarely speak. It is really worth investing some of your valuable space in providing a comfortable harmonious area in which to eat breakfast. After all, our day begins here and we take with us into the world not only the refreshed chi from a good night's sleep, or the "fire" from a warming breakfast, but also the love, support, and encouragement from those around us. Starting from a point of argument or disharmony undoubtedly flavors the rest of the day's experience.

chapter 2

preparing to cook

Meditation: In the beginner's mind there are many possibilities,

but in the expert's mind there are few —Shunryu Suzuki

One of the biggest challenges that we face with cooking is how we prepare ourselves for the adventure. Given that our backgrounds can include the conditioning that cooking is a chore, boring, or a waste of time, it can be difficult to appreciate the possibilities that lie ahead. Somehow, we have to integrate the seemingly paradoxical qualities of yin and yang into our frame of mind when we begin to cook—namely to be relaxed and flexible (yin) while, at the same time, maintaining a sense of focus and purpose (yang).

"being" versus "doing"

One of the most important points to remember when we begin to cook is to leave behind the distractions and day-to-day business of our lives while we pay attention to our cooking. From a yin/yang perspective, our activities, our work, our travel, and our instinctual needs to hunt and gather are all aspects of yang activity. The world of business, our offices and traveling in confined modes of transport all play a part in "yangizing" our conditions and perspectives.

On the other hand, our homes are our retreats, our places of security, where we can relax and recharge our batteries. In this sense, it is a more yin environment, where we can leave behind the aggression and distractions of the outside world and become more yin, but at the same time more vulnerable. Charging into the kitchen, hot off the train, impatient, hungry, and still distracted by the day's business will frequently result in a fast and chaotic meal.

Before we step into the kitchen, it is essential to take a moment to get into yin mode. What are these qualities of yin and yang, and how do they relate to our preparation? Essentially, yang's nature is associated with sunlight, activity, clarity, focus, intention, and speed. Its complementary yet antagonistic partner, yin, can be represented as nighttime, winter, stillness, preparation, reflection, slowness, and as mental rather than physical activity.

These yin and yang qualities can also be related to our chi energies—our vibrations, our spirits. Being highly charged or defensive after dealing with the outside world turns our chi into yang mode, and as we enter into the world of cooking we need to bring in more yin qualities to center ourselves for the tasks in hand. How can we change our chi relatively quickly and easily?

One way to rid yourself of the influence of the chi of your busy day is to take a shower or bath. Another way would be to change your clothes, as the light, vibrational quality of chi attaches itself to this outer, softer layer. Another way to quickly adapt your chi is to create a more yin environment at home or in the kitchen by softening the lighting, playing gentle music, bringing more fresh air into the space, or perhaps lighting a candle. In addition to these suggestions, of course, you could spend a few minutes sitting peacefully in meditation, allowing the day's cares to leave your mind and allowing you to become calm and collected before you begin preparing a meal.

Getting yourself into this state of "being" rather than "doing" is an essential step in succeeding with this approach to cooking. After all, 90 percent of Zen cooking is intuitive. While you get used to this new approach, try to keep everything you do simple and, most important of all, regard it as a learning experience. If a dish burns or tastes disappointing, think about what there is to learn from the experience. It is through continual practice that we begin to develop a true sense of freedom in harnessing fire to transmute food into our blood, our chi, our spirit.

Part of the excitement of beginning anything new is to be pleasantly surprised by the unexpected. However, there is some wisdom in having a clear sense of purpose in what you would like to achieve from this new approach to cooking, together with knowing what your commitment will entail.

The following steps will help in preparation for this approach to cooking, and I recommend you take a month putting it into practice.

1

the vision ahead

Before setting out on any voyage, long or short, it is important to have a sense of where you are trying to go to. For this first step, I suggest that you take a moment to sit quietly and follow a simple meditation process in order to see ahead to one month from now. It may sound difficult but it is really very easy.

Find a comfortable chair or sit in your favorite meditation position on the floor, and narrow your eyes so that they are almost closed. Breathe gently from your belly allowing some three to four seconds to breathe in, hold it for a further three to four seconds, then exhale slowly through your nose with your tongue lightly touching the roof of your mouth for six to seven seconds. Gently settle into this pattern for two or three minutes and allow your thoughts to wander in and out of your mind freely without feeling any attachment to their meaning. Now you will begin to breathe in a more relaxed fashion, unaware of your attempt to breathe in a particular way. Allow any image to appear in your mind which you think represents you a month from now. Feel free to let your imagination come into play and dwell on the positive side of your new-found health, contentment, self-expression, flexibility, and serenity.

Let yourself dwell on any such image for a few minutes. As you breathe in, concentrate on the positive aspects of how you see yourself, and allow this glimpse of the future to transform into chi, into breath, and to permeate your whole being. Feel the warmth of your new self filter out from your chest to your head, to your arms and hands, your belly, legs, and feet.

Slowly allow your awareness to return to the room and, as soon as you can, jot down two or three striking images you recall from the experience. These images provide the essence of your vision of the outcome of this thirty-day experience in discovering a whole new side to cooking, and the preparation and sharing of food.

2

the commitments

It is all well and good having an inspiring vision of what is possible, but what can you do about it now? We all know that it is not always the goal of our journey that rewards us but the journey itself. On a practical level you need to clarify in your own mind the basic commitment that you are going to make on a daily basis which will allow you, step by step, to achieve the dream [OK?] you saw in the visualization process. Here are a few practical suggestions, but of course feel free to design your own.

• **cook a meal for yourself each day** With no particular menu, recipe, or ingredient suggested, I wish you simply to commit yourself to spending time preparing a meal once a day for yourself over the next month. On a busy day, the meal could be breakfast; on the weekend, it could be far more elaborate. The commitment is the important thing.

• **keep your food simple** Rather than feeling overwhelmed by a vast, new shopping list containing strange and exotic ingredients, why not rely on a few basics and learn to use them creatively? I recall vividly that when I began to eat only natural foods my friends and family immediately began to sympathize by saying how boring it must be to rely on so few ingredients. What they did not realize was that by using our intuition we rarely cook the same meal twice, even though the ingredients might be the same. These well-meaning friends who felt sorry for me would likewise receive sympathy from me when I looked at their food. On a fairly regular basis they ate the same meals—fish on Friday, spaghetti on Saturday, roast chicken on Sunday, cold chicken salad on Monday, pork chops on Tuesday, and so on. They all had a limited repertoire and, inevitably, when I ate with them in a restaurant they would choose the same items time and again.

• **try new ingredients.** This could be the perfect time to introduce new ingredients, cooking styles, and recipes that you have been meaning to use for some time. This might mean a switch to using only natural ingredients, certified organic products, or foods that are not genetically modified. It could easily be a shift toward a new hot beverage to replace your old "fix" of caffeinated tea or coffee. If you are fond of meat, you could avoid it for the thirty-day period, and eat fish instead.

- **get up early** Whenever we take on a new commitment or project it can easily consume our time and our passion. This is the ideal time to make that extra effort to get up earlier and to treat the preparation of breakfast and a lunchbox for work as part of your daily meditation. After a few days of making this extra effort the results will begin to pay off. The dawn represents the chi of new beginnings and the element Wood (tree), which is symbolic of new shoots and growth in Chinese medicine.

- **reduce certain foods** Maybe this is the time in your life when you will consciously decide to remove or reduce certain ingredients that you have been worrying about but have not made the effort to act on as yet. It may not be wise to make radical changes, but you may make a conscious effort, for example, to avoid sugar or any foods containing sugar; or to avoid all animal food, including poultry and eggs; or to try to reduce your intake of dairy-based products.

You could also make a list of foods that you crave and eat regularly, and which, if you were to exclude them, could give you valuable insight into why you have these desires in the first place. Such cravings could include caffeine, chocolate, ice cream, orange juice, alcohol, and carbonated beverages.

• **host a meal for others** One of the most valuable forms of feedback on our cooking is criticism from our peers, friends, or family. Without making it into a big deal, invite a few guests and prepare a meal for them—without lecturing them on the benefits of your new-found ingredients and cooking styles. Simply prepare the meal with love, set the tone of the room using the Feng Shui principles outlined in Chapter One, and listen for any comments.

• **eat out once a week** Naturally, if we eat only the food we have prepared ourselves, using our familiar ingredients and seasonings, our outlook and perspective on what is possible can become limited. You may feel during your practice of Zen cooking that you need to keep dedicated to practicing it. I believe that it is vital from time to time to try something completely different and unfamiliar to you. To make sure that your meal out is not a hit or miss affair here are a few tips. Choose a restaurant that you are not familiar with, but has been recommended by a friend. Go for quality rather than quantity. Ask the waiter what the chef is renowned for. Chew the meal very, very well. With an open heart, begin to appreciate the different colors, tastes, and textures of the food. Notice how it is presented and the restaurant's decor and atmosphere. What can you learn?

cooking as

self-expression

We all express ourselves through creative acts and cooking is certainly no exception. Our vitality, our mood, our love, our patience, our chi is all transferred to the food itself, the cooking, and the result. When I first studied macrobiotic cookery with Japanese teachers, it was initially difficult to understand what they were doing. Naturally, there was a language barrier, but I was poised, like others, with notepad and pencil to take down weights, measures, and cooking times. Our frustration was not eased when the cook said that she did not know how much water was in the pot or how much salt she used or how many ounces or grams of seaweed went into a particular dish. "Watch, wait, and taste," was frequently the only answer she would give. Those students who did turn into excellent cooks did so largely by learning through assisting these cooks. Given seemingly menial tasks, such as washing and scrubbing the vegetables, or rinsing the rice or, if they were lucky, the responsibility of roasting sesame seeds, they had opportunities to work with the cooks and begin to understand how they operated.

story

In the 1970s, I lived what I can only call a monastic experience while I was enrolled to study Shiatsu and Macrobiotics at the East West Center in London. I held several daytime jobs to support myself, one of which was in the East West Natural Food Shop on Old Street. There I spent a few hours every day making sandwiches. The task seemed pretty simple—all I had to do was to make twenty rounds of savory seitan sandwiches for lunchtime customers. Seitan is a Japanese product. It is the glutinous part of the wheat transformed through a dough-making process into a delicious meat-like product. It lends itself well to soups and stews and can be deep-fried as a schnitzel or, as in this case, a sandwich filling. Many newcomers to vegetable proteins have been surprised at its texture and flavor, and have mistaken it for real meat. Traditionally, seitan was one of the staple foods of sumo wrestlers during the era when the Japanese largely abstained from eating foods derived from animals.

I would simply slice freshly baked sardo bread; spread on a little tahini and mustard; add a small amount of lettuce, a few slices of dill pickle, and a few strips of seitan and wrap it all up in cling wrap. After doing this for about a week, my enthusiasm began to wane and the manager dropped in on my "production line" to ask if I had been putting an invitation in the sandwiches. It turned out that his baffling request referred to the fact that in recent days fewer and fewer people had been buying the sandwiches. Although the quality was perfect, the product was not "inviting" customers to buy them.

In his own beautifully poetic Irish way, Donald then explained that while I was making the sandwich I needed to concentrate on inviting a purchaser. Still slightly baffled by this new idea, I gave it a shot and to my utmost surprise the sandwiches disappeared off the counter during lunch. I believe that by doing this I learned the first step on the Eightfold Path—"right thought."

tips for developing self-expression

in cooking

- **minimize the use of recipes** As a result of domestic science classes in schools, cooking has come to rely heavily on weights, measures, and volumes, the nutritional breakdown of ingredients, and precise times of cooking. Cooking is essentially an artform and our great-grandmothers would have great difficulties today trying to tell us how much flour they used or the precise temperatures at which they prepared particular dishes.

Like me, you may have managed to acquire a recipe from your mother or grandmother that holds a special place in your heart. Following their instructions fastidiously, did you not feel disappointed when the dish failed to taste as you remember it? There was something special missing. This ingredient "X" was their love, their chi, and any method that was hard to define in writing.

• be aware of your current chi

In recent years a system of recording the aura or charge of chi energy has been developed. It is possible to have the palms of your hands photographed using Kirlian photography, and this reveals haloes of energy emanating from your fingertips and thumbs. An experienced practitioner can then assess your current levels of chi and make suggestions to balance or strengthen it. I saw an example once of a Kirlian photograph of some leaves on a tree, followed by another photograph of the same leaves of which one had been removed just thirty seconds earlier. Despite the leaf's absence, there was still an outline of where it had been, showing that the aura was still present. It would be

relatively
easy to photograph two
different dishes in this manner. One
could be largely made up of organic natural
foods, and the other one perhaps of processed
foods. I am sure that the auras would be sharply
different. A fascinating experiment would be to provide
two cooks with exactly the same ingredients and ask them
to prepare the same dish and then look at the difference. In
scientific terms they should be identical, and contain the
same nutritional value. However, I am convinced that the
chi energy of the cook would be transmitted to the
food and that the auras would vary. Tired cooks
make tired food, hurried cooks make hurried
food—certainly happy cooks make
memorable meals.

• **trust the process** As with any other skill that we develop in life, remaining undaunted in the midst of the process is important. Whenever I take apart any mechanical gadget in an attempt to repair it, I feel overwhelmed by all the bits and pieces, and I wonder if I can ever put it back together again. Skilled engineers seem to follow their own set of rules at work, cutting corners, leaving all the parts in disarray, yet exuding a quiet confidence that they know how to put everything back together again.

Inevitably, when you begin to prepare food with unfamiliar ingredients, often with longer cooking times, and perhaps in less water than usual or with tight-fitting lids to prevent you from seeing what is happening, you can become anxious. Try to avoid the constant temptation to lift the lid off the pot, to adjust the flame every few minutes, and to stir the ingredients to see if they are cooking—all this worry and agitation will be transferred to the chi of the meal. What always amazes me working alongside professional cooks is their capacity to be completely calm at the center of what appears to be chaos.

Annually a colleague of mine would cater annually for summer camps both in Europe and the United States with numbers of participants ranging from five hundred and nine hundred. Supported by a small army of volunteers and surrounded by crates of vegetables and sacks of grains and beans, Howard remained totally calm. Despite having to order all the food, organize the work crews, design the menus and deal with any logistical problems that might arise, Howard always focused on one area. Whenever you called in to see him in the kitchen he was preoccupied with his contribution to the meal, the rice. Hours before the meal was due, the rice had been washed and was sitting in vast stainless steel pots ready to be cooked. Bringing these quantities of rice up to the boil can take an hour or more. Howard was always seen hovering near the pot, never interfering with it, but silent and ever present. In all the years that I ate his food at these camps I never experienced grain that was undercooked, burnt, or soggy.

• **"be in the moment"** In Zen cooking, the preparation and serving of a meal is like a meditation. If you value devoting some time every day to meditation or self-reflection, then you can save time by including cooking as part of your spiritual practice. Without the distractions of the TV, radio, or telephone, you have the opportunity to reflect on who you are cooking for, and what kind of chi you would like to energize the food with. You can and even visualize the outcome of the meal. Given our current busy lifestyles, time is probably our most precious commodity, and real benefits are to be had through this approach of combining meditation with realizing how important food is to us. As with meditation, tai chi, or yoga, food preparation also requires that you "be in the moment."

• **suspend judgement** It is all too easy when acquiring a new skill to become totally immersed in the subject. Like any passion in life, cooking can take up all of your time but at an early stage you inevitably know very little. From this position we often like either to tell everyone how brilliant it is or to condemn other approaches. Both of these expressions are defensive and likely to distance others from you, especially those who know you well and can remember you a few years ago eating a good steak or enjoying bowls of ice cream.

I remember the horror I felt when my parents came to visit shortly after I had begun to use grains and vegetables as the basis of my diet and I found my mother preparing bacon and eggs in my best cast iron skillet! At the time it felt like sacrilege that these kinds of foods were even in my home, let alone being prepared in my best pan. Luckily, I gave no expression to such arrogance to my mother, and with more experience and practice my attitude became more flexible. I remember three years later standing in exactly the same spot, using precisely the same ingredients and "sacred" pan to prepare breakfast for my father-in-law. Although I did not eat the food myself, I was now coming from a sense of hospitality, love, and acceptance of what he wanted.

There is always a sense of curiosity in light of your new discoveries about cooking when you come once again to prepare foods that you used to eat years ago.

I am glad that there are a few certitudes that I have learned during my life of traveling, cooking, and teaching: first, any ingredient is edible, and second, like me, the ingredients all share the same source—this planet. What I have learned to appreciate over the years is that we all have access to an enormous number of choices and it is simply up to us to decide what we wills choose according to our needs. Developing a flexible approach to your cooking will reward you much more than keeping a rigid or dogmatic one.

• **avoid cooking when angry** Cooking for other people and providing them with new blood and refreshed chi is a great honor. But your choice of ingredients and cooking style form only part of the equation–your chi permeates the meal as well. In a subtle way, your thoughts, your feelings and overall vitality get transmitted to the food and, in turn, are reflected in your guests' thoughts and actions a few hours later. In the former Yugoslavia, they have an old folk which says "What you eat today, talks tomorrow."

"Do not seek the
only cease to

truth
cherish opinions"

—Zen saying

story

I had the experience several years ago of attending a spiritual retreat where one of the conditions was that we only ate brown rice and miso soup for the four days of the stay. We were also requested to chew each mouthful of rice between eighty and two hundred times. It sounds like a tall order, but when you only have rice to eat it is worth making a meal of it.

After two days and finally managing to get up to eighty chews per mouthful, I felt surprisingly full and satisfied at the end of a forty-five minute meal in silence. By the fourth day, I had discovered new levels of sensitivity and appreciation about what I was eating. Even though each meal was based on brown rice, each one had a different taste and left me with a different experience.

On the final day my thoughts began to drift toward Bob and how he was managing to prepare this food in the kitchen. I kept thinking about him during the meal and sensed that something was not quite right. I had no idea whether there was any truth in this, but I put my head around the door of the kitchen after the meal. I thanked him for what he had prepared and asked him how he was getting on. It turned out that he had had real difficulties that morning with the ancient and temperamental coal-fired range on which he prepared the rice. The flame either went out, or he was unable to regulate the heat properly, both of which caused him a great deal of anxiety as the rice was our only source of sustenance.

4

grace, prayer, and appreciation

I set out when I was seventeen years old to work and travel my way around the world. After six years I had traveled through fifty-two countries on four continents, and I had always eaten or prepared whatever was local, seasonal, or available. The factor common to all the cultures where I was a guest was that the meal began with some form of appreciation or grace. It was usually nothing elaborate, but at least a few moments were taken either to thank the cook, or thank God for the food, or to wish good health on the people who were about to eat it.

Try taking a few moments before your next meal to bring the palms of your hands together with your fingers touching (prayer posture), and to take a moment to reflect on the origin of the food, the cook, and the refreshment that your chi is about to receive. It need not be an elaborate affair, but simply a connection with what you are about to eat.

I believe that the highest level of appreciation that you can give any cook is to eat everything that you are given. As a cook that says more to me than any number of words. However, it can be challenging to face a meal being cooked for you by a host who is unaware that you may be eating "differently" right now.

This issue came up for me many times when I began to eat vegetarian and vegan foods. I recall being asked on more than one occasion what I would like for dinner as my hosts had heard that I was eating "funny" foods now. I would frequently run through what I would not like to eat and add that I would be happy with brown rice, vegetables, or perhaps some fish.

Inevitably the meal was a bit of a disaster. To begin with, my hosts had attempted to cook something unfamiliar to them, my special needs placing them under considerable pressure. All this anxiety, of course, went into the meal as well. Frequently I would chew my way through half-cooked brown rice, a ratatouille made up of all the vegetables that I never ate (tomatoes, zucchini, eggplant), whereas my hosts' meal looked extremely appetizing. They had cooked their meal with skill, practice, and experience—and, of course, love. After these experiences, I learned to make only a simple request: that I would prefer not to eat meat or sugar.

story

I have discovered that if you avoid prejudging the situation when you enter a new restaurant or travel to a new locale, then you will inevitably find what you need. I no longer travel with bags full of my staples in fear that I will not find what I need. Being flexible, adaptable, and ultimately appreciative of whatever sustenance we are given is the secret.

I was given a real lesson in appreciation by one of my teachers, Mr. Kushi, in 1987. It was late one Sunday night in London and, after a day of teaching and meetings, we went in search of a restaurant. On Sunday nights in London, especially after 11 P.M., it is a challenge to find any restaurants worth their salt. I was ashamed around midnight to have to admit defeat, when Mr. Kushi spotted a late-night pasta bar and pizzeria. I was horrified at the thought of having to take him there, but it seemed the only option. Here were two individuals, who never ate dairy food or refined carbohydrates, about to enter a late-night, fast food restaurant. It was not only an education but an eye-opener in the art of appreciation.

Full of politeness, Mr. Kushi asked if we could have some plain pasta, some black olives in a separate dish, a small bowl of anchovies, and four cups of plain hot water. Mr. Kushi's unusual request was accepted without any problem, and before long we had two plates of steaming, fresh pasta in front of us. Mr. Kushi then soaked the anchovies in one cup of hot water and the olives in the other cup to remove the salt and some of the oil. Without any fuss, he drained them and chopped them on his side plate and stirred them into our pasta. He held his hands in prayer posture and encouraged me to begin the meal, which we both chewed very slowly interspersed with comments of how delicious it was. At the end of the meal, he repeatedly thanked helpful waiter, and left a tip that was almost equal to the value of our simple fare. It was certainly an experience in appreciation and one that left me confident that not only can we eat any food, but, if we suspend our judgement about food and appreciate its qualities, it can always sustain us.

⑤
choosing your

As discussed in Chapter One, the priority with Zen cooking is your state of being, followed closely by having a kitchen that supports you in being able to cook intuitively. The next priority is to select the tools of your trade. The implements that a cook guards closely, and rarely lets anybody else use, are their knives.

cooking utensils

vegetable knife I highly recommend the Japanese vegetable knife known as the hocho, which is extremely sharp. In Japan, these knives are traditionally made by the same producers that make the world-famous samurai swords. The same precision, effort, and delicacy of production all go into the creation of the hocho. Lke the Chinese equivalent, which is bigger and heavier and appears more like a meat cleaver, the hocho can initially seem unwieldy. However, with practice it is extremely delicate and precise. Protect it well, and certainly guard against other cooks in the kitchen using your hocho as a meat cleaver for deboning their chicken! It occurred to me to use it for this purpose once, and the knife was left with large pieces of the delicate blade missing.

Keeping the hocho sharp is an art in itself. Placing a cloth underneath the knife to prevent it from slipping and sliding, hold the blade at a fifteen degree angle to the whetstone, and with the front of the knife positioned higher up the stone than the base, gently rotate the blade in a clockwise, then counterclockwise, direction several times. Only sharpen the reverse side briefly, also at a 15 degree angle to the stone. If you do not have a whetstone, simply use the base of any bowl with an unglazed surface. Dampen the base and rotate the knife blade in the same way against the pottery.

chopping board You will also need a strong, unvarnished, wooden chopping board, preferably at least one inch thick, and a damp cloth for wiping the blade and the board between preparation processes.

scrubbing brush To prepare vegetables before cooking, give them a good scrub with a Japanese, natural bristle brush known as a *tawashi*. Peeling vegetables removes the protective outer layer which contains some of the more yang minerals. A good scrub keeps the vegetables whole, and the bristles get into all the nooks and crannies.

mortar and pestle Also useful in the kitchen is an earthenware mortar which has a serrated inside and a wooden pestle. The mortar is known as a *suribachi* and can be used for crushing roasted seeds, making purées, and dissolving miso paste into soup broth.

pots and pans As far as pots are concerned, I recommend having several on hand. You will need a few heavy pots and a few lighter ones. For soups, stews, casseroles, and grains, you should have at least one cast iron pot, an enameled cast iron pot, a stainless steel pot with a heavy base, and a stainless steel pressure cooker, which is extremely useful for grains or legumes. A heavy-based cast iron skillet with a tight-fitting lid is useful for dry roasting and for slowly sautéing vegetables. For quicker forms of cooking and deep-frying, you can use a stainless steel wok.

strainers I suggest you have at least one large, fine-meshed strainer for washing seeds, beans, and grains, and another one of a similar size, but with a wider mesh, for sieving vegetables and noodles. An almost flat stainless steel oil strainer is ideal for removing pieces of tempura while deep-frying and I would highly recommend a heat disperser to place underneath heavy pots to prevent burning when you are cooking casseroles or grains for a long time on a low heat.

utensils As far as cooking implements are concerned, there is no better feel than the delicate touch of wood. Plastic implements lack chi, and steel implements clash with the iron and steel pans. Keep on hand various wooden spoons, long chopsticks, and a rice paddle carved out of bamboo.

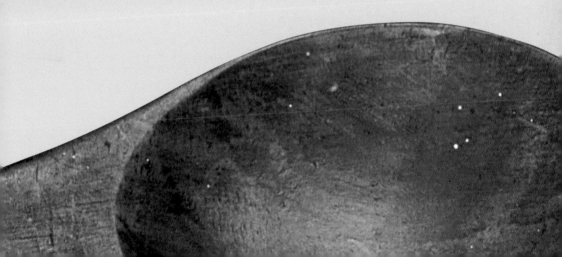

cutting techniques

One of the joys of Zen cooking is learning the different cutting techniques for vegetables. I suggest that you practice on some carrots and onions first.

The strength and chi of your technique does not emanate from your shoulders, wrists, elbows, or even your fingers, but from your belly. In Japan this vital center of our physical being is known as the *hara*. Ideally, your cutting surface needs to be level with your *hara*, which is approximately two finger widths below your navel. If your cutting surface is lower than this, you will tend to stoop and lose focus. If it is higher than this, the muscles of your neck, shoulders, and forearms will become too tight. Begin by breathing from your belly, keep your shoulders and forearms loose, and your grip on the knife handle firm but flexible.

Always keep both hands on the job. In this case, that means one hand on the knife and one hand on the vegetable. To make sure that you leave the kitchen with all the fingers and thumbs that God gave you, hold the vegetable with your knuckles rather than with your fingertips. With your knuckles holding down the vegetable, your thumb can be simultaneously adjacent to the vegetable, and in contact with the chopping board.

When slicing, never draw the blade toward yourself. When chopping, either use direct vertical pressure or allow the furthest part of the blade from the handle to touch the board first and then bring the remainder of the blade down onto the vegetable.

Always remember to wipe the blade and the board before preparing a different kind of vegetable. Keep a series of bowls handy for different vegetables or different shapes of the same vegetable.

Rangiri involves cutting a carrot into triangular chunks or wedges. Begin by holding the carrot with your knuckles and cut an one inch diagonal chunk off the tip. Then gently half roll the carrot and cut off another diagonal piece, half roll it again and cut off another wedge. Continue this process as far as you can toward the top of the carrot. You will now be left with similar-sized triangular chunks of carrot that can be used in casseroles, stews, and soups.

Hasugiri involves cutting a carrot into fairly fine diagonal slices. Again, begin at the tip of the carrot, holding it firmly with your knuckles and allowing the blade to rest against the upright part of your knuckles. Gently press down and cut a slice, simply slide your knuckles further down the carrot as you take off another slice, and so forth.

Sengiri is where you make a pile of three or four hasugiri slices and cut the pile downwards into matchsticks. The width of the cut needs to be equivalent to the depth of the hasugiri slice itself. Again, holding the slices gently under your knuckles allow the blade to rise and fall against the vertical aspect of your knuckles and chop slowly, never letting the blade ride too high up your knuckles.

Like any pruning technique, when you cut a fresh flower on the diagonal it preserves not only the stalk but the chi of the plant in question. Both hasugiri and sengiri, like the rangiri technique help to preserve the chi of the carrot.

Koguchigiri involves cutting very fine cross sections of the carrot. Unlike hasugiri where you sliced through a diagonal, here you simply cut directly across.

Wagiri is the same technique as koguchigiri except you cut the carrot into thicker slices.

Hanjgetsu begins when you remove the top part of the carrot and then slice the carrot from top to bottom into two halves. The second step is to cut each half of the carrot into half moons either finely by koguchigiri, or into thicker chunks by wagiri.

Sainome is a dicing and chopping technique. You can choose between larger or smaller chunks depending on the type of cooking involved. Begin by chopping a medium-sized carrot into thirds. Take one of these pieces and place it vertically on the board. Carefully remove a slither (one-eighth of an inch), cutting away from you as you hold the carrot with your knuckle. This flat section of the carrot will act as a stabilizer as you continue the slicing.

With the carrot in position under your knuckles and with the newly cut flat section firmly in contact with the chopping board take a quarter-inch slice off the section furthest away from you. You are now left with a straight edge and you can chop the carrot into one-eighth or one-quarter inch slices as far as you can safely. Pile up the sections together on the board, and slice them into matchsticks of equal breadth. Keep the pile of matchsticks together and, rotating your knuckles and knife, begin to chop and dice your way down the carrot. It is a very satisfying process and one that I encourage you to practice.

first aid

Please remember, these are very sharp knives. You need not concern yourself about cuts provided you keep your fingertips out of the way and do no allow the blade to rise very high above the vegetable. Over the years, I have had the odd cut and nick due mainly to poor concentration or being distracted while I was chopping. Unless it obviously requires a stitch, the simple solution is to run cold water over the cut and apply pressure to it with a clean cloth for a few minutes. Then, the best remedy I have been taught is to smear a little miso purée on the cut *(miso is salty and can sting)*, and then to cover the cut with a small strip of nori seaweed. This is the same product in which sushi is wrapped and it has the strength to not only bind the cut, but to keep it clean and it also acts as a mild disinfectant.

chapter 3

the alchemy of cooking

Meditation: Not too loose (yin),

not too tight (yang) —Zen saying

One of the secrets of Zen cookery is learning how to transform the ingredients we prepare with the minimum of effort for the maximum effect. Cooking can be intuitive and simple if we work in harmony with the elements involved. Every ingredient and every cooking style has its own yin/yang quality, and in this chapter you will discover how to harness this fundamental knowledge. With a little practice and perseverance, the principles of yin and yang are not difficult to understand and apply practically. In fact, on reflection, it is easy to see that we have been using these principles intuitively throughout our lives.

yin
yang

The vibrational and physical qualities of yin and yang are all around us. Considering that we live in a world that is constantly changing, yin and yang are simple compass bearings that we can use consciously or unconsciously to determine the various stages of change around us and within us. Yin and yang cannot exist separately, and neither can we describe anything as purely yin or yang. We need to have a little of the opposite within us, hence the Daoist yin/yang symbol that evolved to represent this concept.

In ancient times, yang was thought to emanate from above us, in the heavens or from infinity. Conversely, the source of yin was earth itself. From this understanding, yang chi was seen as the force that descends spirally down to earth, whereas yin chi rose spirally from earth to return to infinity.

As yang chi descends, it begins to contract and generate heat, becoming faster and creating natural phenomena such as rocks and minerals that are harder and more durable. Conversely, as yin chi leaves the earth, it becomes more diffused, more expansive, and therefore lighter, softer, and ultimately cooler. When considering the movement of this kind of chi, people associated daytime, the summer, activity, and heat with yang manifestations, whereas nighttime, winter, stillness, and the cold were considered yin qualities.

At their most extreme expressions, yin and yang turn into their opposites. For example, if you feel tired and unmotivated (a yin condition), you could try taking a cold shower (also yin) and the effect would be confronting, invigorating, and awakening, which are all yang qualities. Likewise, with cooking, if you were to apply excessive heat (yang) for a considerable period of time, whatever you cooked would ultimately become diffused or soggy or fall apart (yin) as a result of the extreme heat.

cooking as a "yangizing" process

If you were to look objectively at the cooking process, it is easy to appreciate the yin/yang qualities involved. We begin with cold, fresh ingredients (yin) and apply fire (yang) to them. Whatever cooking style you may wish to apply, this basic flow from yin to yang holds true. Taking a natural cycle, we begin by placing the raw ingredients in cold water and putting them on a flame. This is the ultimate yin phase of cooking as, despite the intense heat that may be under the pot, it has not yet begun to "yangize" the ingredients. The second phase is when the water and the ingredients are hot but not boiling. The third phase is when the water comes to the boil and, in reaching the highest point of heat, represents the most yang phase. The fourth phase is when we turn down the flame a little and allow the ingredients to simmer and settle, and the fifth phase is when we put out the fire completely and allow the pot to cool down and consolidate—"yangizing" the ingredients further.

The whole process complements the traditional use of fire we have used for several thousand years. Beginning with a cold hearth our ancestors would have burned kindling and then larger pieces of wood to get the flames going. Once the flames reached their peak and the ingredients began to boil, the food was simply left to simmer on the hot coals, finally cooling down with the embers. Working effortlessly with this cycle of energy, even with a modern gas flame, helps us to reconnect with the real essence of cooking itself.

the five elements
and their cooking styles

The cycle of yin and yang that occurs on a daily and seasonal basis and within the process of cooking, is regarded as basic theory in traditional Chinese medicine. Zen cooking involves representing aspects of the phases outlined on the opposite page, not only in the preparation of the food but also in its presentation and taste. A meal, as with a work of art, ultimately inspires and uplifts our chi. Traditionally these five phases are associated with the five elements, or forces, recognized in Chinese cosmology as being the formative elements in creation—Water, Wood, Fire, Earth, and Metal.

water This element represents stillness, reflection, the winter, and deeply preserved chi. Like the winter, all may seem quiet and still, but the chi is deep and hidden and being regenerated. The colors are black and deep blue; the time of day is the night; the emotions are courage and perseverance; and the flavor is salty.

Cooking styles	raw, marinading, light pickling

wood This element, or phase, represents new beginnings and the spirit of youth and new-found energy. The chi is active, exploratory, and fresh. Seasonally it is represented by spring; the colors are various shades of green; the time of day is the dawn; the emotions are humor and patience; the flavor is sour.

Cooking styles	quick boiling, quick steaming, blanching, pan frying

fire This element represents inspiration, insight, activity, heat, and passion. It is the ultimate uplifting phase within the five elements. Seasonally it is represented by the summer; the colors are red, purple, mauve, pink and violet; the time of day is noon; the emotions are passion, laughter, and warmth; the flavors are bitter.

Cooking styles	deep frying, wok style

earth When Fire dies down it gives way to ashes. This phase represents the settling and nurturing qualities of Earth, a slowing down, and gentle, mellow kind of chi. Its season is represented by the late summer; the colors are yellow, orange, gold, and cream; the time of day is the afternoon; the emotions are empathy, care, and concern; the flavors are sweet.

Cooking styles	sautéing, short casserole dishes, long boiling

metal At this phase, chi energy condenses and becomes more durable. It represents the ultimate consolidation within the five phases. Seasonally this is the autumn; the colors are whites and silver; the time of day is evening; the emotions are feeling enthusiastic and positive; the flavors are pungent or spicy.

Cooking styles	baking, roasting, long-term pickling, pressure cooking, and longer versions of steaming

the five-phase support cycle

Each of these phases naturally supports the other. Water is the mother of Wood, which represents plant life. Wood is the mother of Fire, which, in turn, gives way to ashes and soil. As this Earth phase consolidates, it becomes rock and minerals, represented by the element Metal. In time, and under pressure, the rock liquefies, turning into a plasma-like substance which gives rise to the phase Water.

As in traditional Chinese medicine, if one of the elements becomes highly charged or out of control it ceases to support its "child," the next element in the cycle, and cuts across the cycle destroying, damaging, or controlling the opposite element.

the control cycle can be represented by the following traditional model

water puts out fire

fire melts metal

metal chops wood

wood (as in the roots of plants) breaks up earth

earth dams or absorbs water

these phases can be associated with cooking

too much water If we continually use too much water in our cooking the food can turn out limp and soggy. The ultimate expression of the Water phase would be eating raw food exclusively, which would suppress or negate the presence of Fire in the preparation. Too much watery food in general will put out the Fire in our chi.

too much fire Naturally, if we overcook our food then it will take on the qualities of the Metal phase and become dry, burnt, and brittle. A good example of this is burning our bread when we meant to only toast it.

too much metal Overcooking our food ultimately destroys the essence of Wood chi—the freshness that Wood energy brings to our food.

too much wood If our food is consistently cooked for too short a time it does not allow the richness and the mellowness of the Earth element to evolve.

too much earth If we consistently prepare meals that are cooked slowly over a long period of time this style can prevent the "essence," represented by the water element, from coming through. Such a dish is likely to have only one overall flavor and may not reveal the hidden qualities of the different ingredients.

"If you care enough
you will almo

for the result,
st always attain it."

—William James

fire/time/pressure/salt

Balance and harmony in our cooking style involves bringing a variety of these four qualities into the kitchen. Try not to allow your current state or conditioning to lead the way. With a little time and practice it becomes easy to observe if you are getting the right balance in the elements of fire, time, pressure, or salt within your cooking.

fire

If we choose to use no flame at all in our cooking this would represent the ultimate yin phase. Using a high flame naturally brings the yang chi into play. The higher the flame, the more yang the cooking style is; the lower the flame, the more yin the cooking style.

time

The preparation time for any ingredient has yin and yang qualities all of its own. Short, sharp cooking styles are more yin, whereas dishes that take time to prepare and cook are more yang. The extreme yin versions that require no time to cook would obviously be raw foods, and the ultimate yang dishes would be those cooked for six, seven, or eight hours.

pres
sure

Not to be confused with pressure cooking, what is meant here is the pressure that is brought to bear on the food either by having a tight-fitting lid or by cooking it in an oven. We know that pressure is energy, and is therefore yang. If we consistently cook our food without a lid we are missing out on the yang quality that pressure can bring. Conversely, if we prepare each dish in a heavy pot with a tight-fitting lid, or we like to prepare casseroles, or reheat ready-made meals in the oven, then we are bringing into our lives too much of this yang pressure.

salt

This vital mineral has been part of our cooking tradition since time immemorial. Salt represents one of the most yang condensing phases of energy available. Its yang quality allows us to preserve and lock in the vitality of chi in the food that we are preparing. In trading over the centuries, it has, at times, been worth as much as gold. The word "salary" derives from the tradition of paying Roman soldiers in salt instead of coinage. However, as with any powerful element, too much salt can be dangerous; equally, too little or none at all, and our cooking—and consequently our chi—lacks endurance and strength.

story

As a nine-year-old schoolboy, I left my home in tropical Kenya to begin a fresh education in England at a boarding school. From a yin/yang perspective it was quite a shock to my system! Gone were the sunny, bright skies, the warm, sandy beaches so close to our home, and the warm tropical nights. The bright colors, the heat, and the incessant activity of nature are predominantly yang factors. By contrast, everything and everyone in England appeared to be cold and gray; I had entered the yin zone. Gray was the new color I discovered—the sky, the people, the food, and the weather.

To sustain ourselves in the cold, yin parts of the world, we need to increase our use of fire, time, pressure, and salt. Whether our school cooks knew these principles or not, they certainly endeavored to balance the climate with plenty of these factors.

Before dawn you could often catch the smell of porridge wafting up stairways toward the dormitories. Or, if not porridge, then the yang breakfast fare would be fried bread or an over-cooked sausage, or worst of all, an over-cooked kipper. It was usual at breakfast time to smell lunch being prepared with plenty of fire, time, pressure, and salt. The vegetables that they served had lost all signs of yin or freshness as they were reduced to a mushy pulp. Likewise, all the desserts were burdened with fire, time, and pressure. There were lots of apple pies, treacle tarts, and fruit crumbles, but nothing light, crispy, or naturally sweet. There was nothing yin.

Historically, to survive in the cold and damp of northern climes, our forebears needed plenty of fire, time, pressure, and salt in their cooking. Virtually everything they ate was cooked, and for a considerable amount of time—sometimes overnight. Stews and soups were often left on the hearth gaining flavor and strengthening their "yangizing" properties. Baking or roasting were traditional to all these cultures, and most of their dishes were savory, whether cooked or pickled.

Imagine an ancient Scot waking up on a cold, damp morning, faced with the prospect of going fishing or hunting in the rain for the day and only having a cold glass of orange juice to sustain him? No, he would have had a hot bowl of porridge, which had been bubbling away overnight (plenty of fire, time, and pressure), with a sprinkling of salt, rather than the luxury of cream or milk, or two spoonfuls of sugar.

It is important to remember that although these yang qualities can benefit us in fighting the cold (the yin), the prolonged use of yang is ultimately going to make us seek out "big yin." The big yin that every schoolboy colleague of mine gave their life for was candy. The big yin that our Scottish ancestors needed from time to time to rebalance their condition was probably alcohol. Yin and yang ultimately balance us, even if the process is extreme.

variety in cooking

A beautifully proportioned
and balanced meal needs to have
variety throughout. Variety can be seen in terms
of color, taste, texture, flavor, cooking styles,
ingredients, and proportions. As far as cooking styles are
concerned, try to integrate as much variety as possible—with
the least effort—into the preparation of the meal. While a colorful
bowl of freshly plucked salad may seem appealing to the eye, it will
also lack any element of fire, salt, or even softness. At the other end
of the spectrum, an over-cooked vegetable and bean stew together
with soggy grain or noodles will also lack variety and freshness.

Using the five-elements theory, it is possible to distinguish
cooking styles that relate to Water, Wood, Fire, Earth, or Metal.
It is also possible to adjust them slightly through the four
principles presented in the previous section: that is, by
increasing or decreasing the amount of fire,
time, pressure, and salt within your
chosen cooking style.

water-style
cooking

- **eating raw foods:** Include salads and garnishes.
- **marinading:** Soak the ingredients, without pressure, in a liquid that is either brine-based, vinegar-based, or shoyu-based.

wood-style cooking

- **blanching** Simply dip the ingredients into boiling water for anything from ten seconds to two minutes.
- **boiling** Boil the ingredients without a lid for up to six minutes.
- **wok frying** Use a very thin, steel wok set on a high flame, and the ingredients will be cooked in less than six minutes.

fire-style cooking

- **stir frying** Use a heavy, cast-iron pan or skillet on a very high flame and a good quality oil; the ingredients are cooked within six minutes with continued activity (stirring is yang).

  - **deep frying** Use a heavy, cast-iron pot and bring the oil up to a temperature of 350–360 degrees Fahrenheit. Depending on the size of the ingredients to be cooked, the process can last from two to six minutes.

    - **grilling** Use a natural flame at a high temperature to sear the surface of the ingredients. Cooking time is two to six minutes.

earth-style
cooking

- **sautéing** Use a heavy, cast-iron pan or skillet, basted with oil. Stir the ingredients slowly. Occasionally simmer with a heavy lid on top. Cooking time is six to twenty minutes.
- **poaching** Gently steam the ingredients on a low flame for twenty to forty minutes.
- **casserole/stew/nabe** Using a heavy, cast-iron pot (enameled is fine), cook the ingredients on top of the stove for fifteen to thirty minutes. If a casserole is cooked for much longer, for example up to ninety minutes, or cooked in the oven, then the cooking borders on metal style.

metal-style cooking

- **steaming** Steaming vegetables with a lid in place to create an atmosphere of pressure is a metal-style method of cooking. Cooking time is eight to twelve minutes. If it is considerably less than this and without a lid it qualifies more as blanching *(see Wood-Style Cooking)*.

- **smoked products** Smoked raw ingredients are intensely "yangized" in this process. The confinement *(pressure)* of the smoking room together with the smoke *(fire)* and time make this a concentrated metal cooking style.

- **baking, roasting, and pressure cooking** are other metal-style cooking methods.

the yin/yang food spectrum

It is important to develop an understanding in yin and yang terms of the different ingredients that you can use in cooking. If we were to list the different categories of foods in those terms, then the most yin of all consumable substances would be the air that we breathe. Air would be followed by water, then the softer fruits, salads, and vegetables that have a short shelf-life, and finally, toward the yang end of the spectrum, would come the more solid foods that store well, including grains, legumes, pickles, dried fish, dried meat, and various condiments.

Just how well a grain can retain its yang energy is illustrated in the following example. Some years ago an earthenware pot of barley was excavated in an Egyptian pharaoh's burial chamber. It was carbon-dated by scientists to be approximately 4000 years old, and yet was still able to sprout barley. The consolidated yang energy of this grain of barley had the power to lock in its chi—quite the opposite of a mushroom, for example, which is extremely yin and loses its vitality within hours. One of the secrets of the Zen approach to cooking is to be able to select a variety of ingredients, which imbue us with different forms of chi.

It is important when dealing with and preparing very active yin or yang foods to avoid accentuating their quality with a similar cooking style. For example, if you take a salmon which has many yang factors–being an extremely active fish, red-blooded, with enormous stamina to swim upstream and leap waterfalls–and prepare it in a yang fashion by roasting, baking, smoking, grilling, or deep-frying, then you will simply accentuate its nature and may need to compensate with some form of strong yin. Preparing the salmon in a more yin fashion will help to balance its innate chi. Eat it raw (like sashimi) or marinade it, make a short casserole, a gentle sauté, or you could poach it.

yin factors

Yin ingredients include vegetables and salads that grow quickly, plants that grow at night (such as mushrooms, potatoes, and tomatoes), plants that enjoy the heat of strong sunshine, and any ingredient that is highly processed.

Yin ingredients include any food that loses its strength or vitality shortly after harvest, such as peas; those ingredients for which the effect of the food is felt very quickly, for example spice or sugar; and ingredients that have a higher liquid or potassium content. In general, yin-quality foods could be categorized to include the following: fruits, salads, vegetables, dairy products, sugars, spices, processed foods, stimulants, and most beverages.

yang factors

Broadly speaking, yang ingredients will have many of the following factors in common: tendency to grow slowly, preference for colder seasons for growth, more condensed and hard, more likely to be of animal rather than vegetable origin, capacity to store well, slow-burning energy, and generally higher in sodium and lower in liquid content.

In the vegetable world, grains, sea vegetables (seaweed), and legumes have enduring qualities that define them as more yang. Borderline in the vegetable kingdom are roots that can maintain their reserves of chi for six months.

Animal foods such as meat, including poultry, and eggs are regarded as yang. Wild game or dark flesh are more yang than white meat or domesticated fowl, such as chicken. Eggs are the most condensed of all foods, having the embryo and its own life-supporting yolk contained in one unit. The most yang of all eggs are caviar.

Fish, although less yang than meat or fowl, do have their own yin/yang qualities. White meat, shellfish, and slow-moving fish, such as plaice and flounder, are more yin than the red-blooded, more aggressive tuna, salmon, or bonito.

five-element cooking

Here is a simple refreshing meal that is popular in Japan, yet represents many aspects of the cooking styles I have already mentioned. The ingredients, tastes, presentation, and cooking style all show different facets of the five elements.

Water is represented by soba (buckwheat), the sea vegetables in the dashi, and, of course, by the large amount of liquid within the dish. Wood is represented by the scallion garnish and the sour taste of lemon; Fire by the tempura style of cooking; and Earth by the softly cooked vegetables and the sweetness that they lend to the dish. Finally, Metal is expressed most in the time that the dashi takes to prepare and mature, but also in the sprinkling of togarashi pepper which has the pungent flavor of the metal element.

soba noodles Soba noodles are made from buckwheat, which is native to Russia and northern Japan. Sometimes classified as a grain, or at least a primitive grain, buckwheat more likely represents the evolutionary turning point between primitive grasses and the formation of grain that occurred thousands of years ago. In Russia, kasha, a porridge made from buckwheat groats, was traditionally part of the diet before the advent of potatoes in the seventeenth and eighteenth centuries. It is very resilient to the cold, arid climatic conditions in which it grows. Equally, when we eat this more refined version of buckwheat, as soba noodles, it provides us with warmth and stamina.

tempura Every aspect of Japanese cooking is almost clinically clean and free of all fat and oil. Tempura-style cooking actually owes its origins to the visiting Portuguese missionaries and sailors who would batter vegetables or fish and boil them in oil–a cooking style known as tempora. However, the oil and batter are difficult to digest, so the Japanese eat it with a combination of finely grated daikon, shoyu, and a hint of ginger. For the Portuguese it was probably vinegar or young vinegar wine that accompanied the meal. For this version of tempura there is no need to have any dip because the broth and its garnish will fill that role adequately.

Making tempura can initially seem a challenge, but once you have been successful it is very tempting to tempura just about everything! The secret lies in having the temperature hot enough (360°F) and using good quality organic sunflower oil and an excellent batter. In addition, successful deep-frying depends a lot upon your own condition. You are literally playing with fire. If your condition is more yang—active and focused—then you will feel at ease with the process, but if you are feeling tired, unenthusiastic, vulnerable, and lethargic, then the process can seem intimidating, and you may not be prepared to risk boiling the oil on a high enough flame, thus rendering the tempura soggy instead of crispy. In my experience, one could devote a whole book to Zen and the Art of Tempura Making.

tempura soba

serves 4

9 ounces soba noodles
2 ½ quarts water
1 4-inch strip kombu seaweed
5 cups of water
Pinch of sea salt
Half an onion, diced or thinly sliced
1 carrot, sliced diagonally into ¼-inch strips
1 teaspoon dried bonito flakes
Soy sauce (shoyu), to taste
A selection of vegetables and fish for the tempura ingredients
9 ounces plain flour, sieved
12 ounces ice-cold water
1 egg
Organic sunflower oil
Scallions, finely chopped, to garnish
Half a lemon, thinly sliced, to garnish

step one: cooking soba noodles Soba noodles need plenty of water to boil in and adequate room in the pot for them to boil up. I prefer to use noodles that are 40 percent soba as the 100 percent variety takes a long time to cook and often falls apart in the process. Check the packet for a more accurate guide to cooking time as it can vary with their size.

Bring the water to a high boil and slowly allow the raw noodles to melt into the water. Usually there is no need to add any salt as it is present in the noodles themselves. Keep a large mug of cold water handy to douse the noodles with a shock of cold water on at least two or three occasions as they begin to boil over. Toward the end of the cooking time, take out one noodle and check it for consistency before pouring the contents of the pot through a large sieve. Run cold water through them for several minutes, continually stirring them to prevent them from adhering to each other. If you wish to prepare them in advance, cold soba noodles will keep for at least two days in the refrigerator.

step two: making dashi The traditional dashi, or broth, that accompanies tempura soba is extremely simple—consisting of shoyu, a little vegetable stock, or even bonito stock. I prefer a richer stock which can be sieved to provide a clear broth for the noodles.

Place five cups of cold water, with a pinch of salt, in a saucepan. Add the strip of dried kombu seaweed. Bring this to a rapid boil and add the onion. Once the onion has become translucent, add the carrot. Allow the stock to simmer for fifteen minutes and add one teaspoon of dried bonito flakes per cup of broth. Add shoyu to taste. Continue to simmer for three minutes.

Once the tempura is prepared, you can reheat the broth and then sieve it into the bowl on top of the noodles and tempura.

step three: preparing the tempura ingredients You can tempura virtually anything, provided it is cut finely to allow the heat to penetrate the center. To begin with, I recommend ⅛ inch diagonal slices of carrot, ⅛ inch half moons of onion, ⅛ inch slices of orange-fleshed pumpkin *(hokkaido)*, green capsicums cut into eight sections, king prawns peeled but with their tails, and fine slices of flounder, sole, or monkfish.

step four: preparing the batter One of the secrets of a good batter is to use ice-cold water with the binding and "yangizing" qualities that a raw egg can provide. Swiftly beat the flour, ice-cold water, and egg together in a bowl. You can even keep the batter mixture cold by placing two or three ice cubes in it while you prepare the tempura. In a separate bowl, put half a cup of plain flour in which to dip the battered ingredients before dropping them into the oil.

step five: cooking tempura Pour the sunflower oil to a depth of 3 inches into a heavy cast-iron pot, and heat it to about 360° F. *(Use a cooking thermometer to check that the temperature is hot enough.)* If you are unsure of the temperature, allow a few drops of batter to fall into the hot oil. They should sizzle or rise to the surface in a matter of seconds.

Using a pair of long wooden chopsticks, briefly dip the ingredients into the batter. Allow any excess batter to drain off, and then dip the ingredient in the bowl of flour for a little dusting. In rapid succession, dip, batter, dust, and drop the ingredients into the oil. With the long wooden chopsticks make sure that the ingredients are not sticking together. Remove them when they turn golden brown *(after three to five minutes)* and allow them to drain either on absorbent paper toweling or a stainless steel rack. Between each deep-frying session, skim the surface with a stainless steel, flat sieve to remove any excess batter.

presentation Fill the lower third of your bowl with soba noodles, lay on several pieces of tempura, and then pour boiling hot broth on top. To complete the meal, garnish with the scallions—sliced on the diagonal to maintain their freshness—and one very finely sliced half-moon of lemon. You can add a little Japanese pepper, if desired.

storing food

The moment you cook any dish it begins to lose its flavor, its vitality, and its chi. We are all aware that certain dishes retain their flavor better and can be stored longer than others. From a yin/yang perspective, foods prepared in a more yang fashion—with long, slow use of fire—or that consist of mainly yang ingredients *(meat, grains, legumes)*, will keep longer than dishes that are cooked quickly (more yin) or contain more yin ingredients *(mushrooms, capsicums, spring greens)*. The secret lies in prolonging the chi of yang dishes and minimizing the need to preserve any dish with high yin. With skill and practice it is easy to recognize that soups and stews will keep a few days whereas a freshly prepared steamed dish of Chinese cabbage will become limp and low in chi in a matter of minutes.

If you do store cooked dishes in the refrigerator avoid using cling wrap or keeping them in tight-fitting plastic containers. Although these processes reduce the possibility of mold developing, without air the chi will be diminished far quicker. Storing cooked grains in the refrigerator will cause them to dry out, whereas storing freshly cooked noodles in the refrigerator will preserve them for a day or two.

In flower arranging how you cut the stalk of the flower in question impacts how long the flower will last. The whole purpose of flower arranging is to understand how to extend the chi of the flower. In the same way, you must learn how to store food to retain its chi.

A good test for your storage skills is to see how long you can preserve a freshly cooked pot of brown rice. *(See page 178 for the method for cooking brown rice.)* Wait until the pot has cooled down for about an hour. Take a wooden bowl and lightly smear the interior with sesame oil. Taking a bamboo rice paddle, remove a vertical cross-section of the rice from the pot and gently spread it into the base of the bowl. This cross-section represents the lighter, fluffier qualities of the rice that was cooked at the top (yin) and the more condensed, nutty-brown qualities of the rice that was nearer the base (yang). Continue by taking from the pot one vertical section after another of the rice and layering them on top of each other in the bowl. To really preserve the grain for as long as possible, you can put one of the Japanese pickled plums known as umeboshi, into the center of the grain. Umeboshi has extraordinary preserving qualities and a small piece is frequently used at the center of a Japanese rice ball to help extend its shelf life. Complete the storage process by covering the rice bowl with either a bamboo sushi mat or a slightly damp towel. Find the coolest part of the kitchen to store the bowl and do not be tempted to use the refrigerator.

chapter 4

food to suit

Meditation: Tell me, I'll forget. Show me, I may remember.

But involve me and I'll understand. —Chinese proverb

Traditionally the cook in the monastery looked after the health of the other monks. He was able to assess their needs and balanced what he prepared according to the climate, the seasons, and the activities they were likely to be engaged in that day. Like the cook in monastic life, mothers and grandmothers have always held a central position in determining the health and welfare of their families. Their intuitions, developed from years of understanding the preparation of food and the needs of their families, has been powerful. With a combination of love and intuition, they could reward members of their families with a little extra, heartier (yang) portion of the meal, to sustain them when they were tired or recovering from illness.

supporting our lifestyle

Finding the right balance for our lifestyle and supporting it through our diet is essential. Broadly speaking, if we regard our food and its preparation as our fuel, then we need to "burn it" appropriately for our condition and lifestyle. In an ideal world, the fuel we take on board needs to be consumed with the minimum of waste for the maximum efficiency. If you wish to take time out and become a Zen monk for a month then you will inevitably experience difficulties in being in the moment if your condition, caused by your food, becomes too restless or scattered. Meditating peacefully is not easily accomplished when we are fueled by coffee, sugar, spices, or processed foods.

At the other extreme, if you decide to take on heavy manual work and fuel yourself on simple grains and vegetables, you will have the stamina and flexibility but nothing in reserve. If your work involves plenty of interaction with other people—making rapid decisions, involving yourself in debate and negotiations, and meeting deadlines—then you will need fuel that will support your mental and intellectual agility. Trying to have your wits about you is not easy if you have eaten too much heavy food (yang), such as baked potatoes, roast meat, cold sandwiches, pies, and pastries.

Finding this balance between our lifestyle and how we fuel ourselves has become a modern challenge. In the Zen approach, we are encouraged to search for the truth. The process can be frustrating, paradoxical, and challenging, but at least the discoveries we make are unique and our own. Over-eating in relation to what we need for our lifestyle naturally leads to obesity, inactivity, and a lack of true hunger.

Finding the appropriate fuel for our lives is not as challenging as it may sound. Using the basics of yin and yang and Oriental diagnosis, it is quite easy to gain a new perspective on who we are and what we need.

story

In my late twenties, I studied Shiatsu massage at the East West Center in London. Within a couple of years I was given the honor of teaching classes myself and had the opportunity in the United States to study with one of the world's foremost Shiatsu teachers and practitioners, Shizuko Yamamoto. Arriving in New York in the 1950s, Shizuko had initially found work as a cook in a Japanese restaurant. When I met Shizuko she was in her 50s, strong as an ox, and very down to earth. Her diagnosis was always clear and sharp, and she did not mince her words when offering advice or criticism.

When I invited Shizuko to teach my students in London the following year, I discovered her softer side. Having no family or children of her own, she had a tendency to advise people in a direct manner, like parents do when they speak out of unconditional love. The big treat in hosting Shizuko in London was to take her to a fine Japanese restaurant in the evenings. Not only was Shizuko able to cook brilliantly, but she also knew everything about the menu. She guided me around it and explained all the options available.

However, she would rarely let me choose what to eat! I was fairly slim at the time, so she would order massive portions to fatten me up. I made absolutely no complaints since I could rarely afford to visit such an expensive restaurant.

On one occasion, she insisted on ordering me a dish of deep-fried flounder. She declared that I looked low in calcium and that this would do me good. I duly ate the flesh off the flounder, but then she ordered me to eat all the fine bones as well in order to obtain more calcium.

Having done this to her approval, she then thought I should tackle some of the backbone—an even better source of calcium! I struggled through as much as I could and spent much of the next day trying to remove small pieces of bone from between my teeth.

What Shizuko represents to me is that generation who supports you, in an uncompromising fashion, with what is best for you and your health. Rather than spoiling you, they strengthen you through traditional wisdom and intuition regarding food and its preparation, matching this with your needs and condition.

our condition reflects our cooking

From an Asian perspective, our condition—our health—is created by the intake of the following: food, liquid, air, and chi energy. These four factors are responsible, in varying degrees, for the creation of our blood and our expression of health. Rather than looking for symptoms on the surface of imbalances in our condition, traditional doctors would always be looking for the root cause. Food, along with our liquid intake, was high on the priority list.

Food is obviously crucial to our life support, but at the same time, of all the four factors mentioned above, we can live the longest without it. It was not uncommon for Zen monks to fast for thirty to forty days to achieve new levels of enlightenment. Liquid is far more important to us in terms of our daily survival. Without adequate intake we are severely ill within five to six days. And without air we are unable to survive more than three or four minutes. What about chi energy? In essence this is the Life Force, and we receive this charge not only through our breath, our liquid intake, and our food, but also from our immediate environment, the changing seasons, and the love and support we receive from those around us.

Liquid, air, and chi, though vital for our survival, are not always under our control. We have little choice over the air we breathe, or the quality of water that the rain or waterways provide for us. Nor can we control the seasons, the weather, the chi of our home, or the expressions of love and support from those around us. The one area we can control and for which we have total responsibility is our food and our cooking. We can choose the ingredients, how to prepare them, and how much to eat, and we can decide whether or not to prepare them ourselves. It is in making these decisions that we make the vital link between real, conscious cooking and our health.

It is also important to remember that our condition, like the world in which we live, is constantly changing. By reassessing our condition from time to time we enable ourselves to adapt our diet and lifestyle to support us. Rather than rigidly eating the same meals, drinking the same beverages, and taking the same form of exercise day in and day out, it is wise to take stock of our current condition occasionally and see how we can balance it. As we get used to eating and living in a certain pattern, it becomes ingrained in our condition and colors how we experience the world. The net result is that we perpetuate any minor imbalance in our health and our condition through our cooking.

If our condition becomes predominantly yin we are likely to feel:

- tired
- lethargic
- unenthusiastic
- anxious
- secretive
- sensitive

aspects of a yin condition

aspects of a yang condition

In a more yang state we are likely to feel:

- hyperactive
- aggressive
- competitive
- impatient
- adventurous
- insensitive

yin/yang balance and attraction

One of the problems with finding any form of yin/yang balance is that our condition (whether more yin or more yang) will always determine what we feel we need and the foods we desire. Inevitably, if our condition remains more yin or more yang for any length of time, we will desire similar qualities of foods, activities, and cooking styles. All this is doing is perpetuating the imbalance. If you can imagine attending a cocktail party where initially everyone is mingling together, there comes a time in the evening where various cliques appear. From a yin/yang perspective the yin characters are in deep discussion with other yin people, and the yang ones are grouped on the other side of the room.

The yin group may prefer to sit down, discuss art, poetry, relationships, and open up to other yin individuals. On the other hand, the yang characters are often standing, discussing sports, politics, and work in a fairly superficial, but loud and aggressive fashion. Subconsciously, the yang group may look over at the yin group and think that they need a bit more fire, expressiveness, passion—and a good steak! Conversely, the yin group will regard them as insensitive, noisy, boisterous, and wish that they would quiet down. In reality, both groups would benefit by spending time with each other and learning about the opposite qualities of their current condition.

yin attractions

foods sweet, spicy, soft, creamy, and juicy foods.

activity leisurely or solitary pursuits, quiet activities.

cooking raw, cold, and ready-made foods; sandwiches, snacks, and fruits.

yang attractions

foods savory, well-cooked, crunchy, or dry.

activities vigorous, competitive, team sports.

cooking food cooked with a high flame, quickly prepared, crispy.

Pursuing a path of spiritual enlightenment may easily be regarded as a yin manifestation. Plenty of reflecting, with an absence of mind and little breath are fundamentally yin qualities. But visit any monastery, and you will find that this refined yin lifestyle is balanced by some very down-to-earth yang activities. It is "yangizing" and shocking to be roused from your sleep at 4 A.M., the cold and the stillness of meditation are "yangizing," the poverty and simplicity of the lifestyle is equally "yangizing," and the bursts of vigorous activity such as cleaning are all profoundly yang. In any situation there needs to be balance. The more our diet, lifestyle, or condition veers in one direction, the more we are attracted to, or forced to face, the opposite form of chi to regain balance. This can be done consciously or in extreme situations by accidents which wake us up and reveal the reality of the situation.

"Again and again, look

within thine own mind."

—Padma-Sambhava

asian diagnosis

Diagnosis forms the cornerstone of all Asian healing systems. Through its practice, an acupuncturist, an herbalist, or Shiatsu therapist is able to determine not only whether your current condition is more yin or more yang, but which organ and its supportive element needs attention. It is a fascinating study and one that, with practice, can reveal potential strengths and weaknesses in all of us.

The essence of all Asian medicine is prevention. In the West, we have a tendency to be experts at fixing things once symptoms or imbalances have occurred. Traditionally in China you paid regular visits to your acupuncturist while you were healthy to maintain good equilibrium. If you became seriously ill, it was questionable that you should even pay your practitioner.

Based on a diagnosis, a course of treatment would be offered which could include acupuncture, herbs, massage, dietary advice, and lifestyle suggestions. My dream would be to see a Zen restaurant where you did not choose what to eat but the chef decided for you! Rather than being clinical in this approach, it is hoped with the ideas and exercises in this section that you will be able to develop a more intuitive understanding of how to integrate these basic principles into your life. By getting a "fix" on your current condition you can then adjust your diet and lifestyle accordingly.

Try not to be overwhelmed by the clinical connotation of the word "diagnosis." All of us have been assessing and diagnosing others all our lives. It is part of our intuitive make-up. Notice how you assess a friend or a relative subconsciously when you have not seen them for a long time. With the polarity of time and space between you, when you meet you have a whole new, fresh perspective on the person. In this instance you are judging them on many different levels. "They look tired." "They look older." "They look brighter." "They look bouncy." "They appear impatient." "They look drained." "They are happy." "Is there something bothering them?" In those first few seconds of being reunited with someone you know, a lot of information is being transmitted to you.

As you immerse yourself in conversation and their emotions and share your experiences, you lose these perceptions. In the same vein, it is difficult to diagnose those you see every day, and the biggest challenge of all is yourself. The familiarity of your own energy and that of those around you makes it virtually impossible to sense it intuitively. However, there are a few simple exercises that can be drawn from traditional Asian diagnosis which are easy to apply. It is important not to become neurotic about this, but to reflect, perhaps seasonally, on what changes you may need to make in your cooking and lifestyle. Remember, you have used much of this material in your life without ever labelling it or calling it diagnosis. With a little time and practice you can use these skills.

are you yin or yang today?

The exercise on the next two pages is designed to help you assess briefly whether your *current* condition is more yin or more yang. Only check the box for each question or statement if you identify with it. If you do not, then ignore it. At the end of the exercise, simply add up how many yin and how many yang symptoms you have and see if the equation is one sided.

If by chance your answer results in an equal number of yins and yangs, then use the following "tie-breaker" question, which can tip the balance either way: Using the back of your hand, gently feel the palm of your other hand and notice whether it feels dry or moist. Dry is more yang, moist is more yin. It is an accurate assessment of your current state.

It is important to remember that whatever assessment you make of your condition today, it can easily change to the opposite tomorrow. Do not leave the exercise thinking for ever after that you are yin! The purpose of the exercise is simply to get a "fix" on where your condition is today. This will help in the next section where you can look at your lifestyle and cooking to help pull your condition in the opposite direction.

- ❑ Is your skin oily? (Yin)
- ❑ Is your skin dry? (Yang)
- ❑ Do you have watery eyes? (Yin)
- ❑ Do you have dry or itchy eyes? (Yang)
- ❑ Is your hair currently oily or limp? (Yin)
- ❑ Is your hair currently dry or brittle? (Yang)
- ❑ Is your urine clear? (Yin)
- ❑ Is your urine dark? (Yang)
- ❑ Do you tend to sleep for eight hours or more? (Yin)
- ❑ Do you tend to sleep for six hours or less? (Yang)
- ❑ Are you currently craving sweet, spicy, or creamy food? (Yin)
- ❑ Are you craving dry, well-cooked, or savory foods? (Yang)
- ❑ Have you recently felt anxious, fearful, or depressed? (Yin)
- ❑ Have you recently felt excitable, irritable, or aggressive? (Yang)
- ❑ Do you easily bruise? (Yin)
- ❑ Do you have a tendency to get a stiff neck? (Yang)
- ❑ Do you prefer long, hot baths? (Yin)
- ❑ Do you prefer short, cooler, showers? (Yang)
- ❑ Do you tend to walk slowly and meander? (Yin)
- ❑ Do you walk fast and purposefully? (Yang)

- ❏ While driving do you give way easily to other drivers? (Yin)
- ❏ While driving do you get frustrated and impatient with the traffic? (Yang)
- ❏ Is your idea of relaxation a quiet evening alone with a book? (Yin)
- ❏ Is your idea of relaxation a wild evening out with friends? (Yang)
- ❏ Do you tend to ponder or procrastinate? (Yin)
- ❏ Do you prefer to get straight to the point? (Yang)
- ❏ Do you dislike extremes of hot or cold weather? (Yin)
- ❏ Does the heat or cold not affect you? (Yang)
- ❏ Does everyone seem faster than you? (Yin)
- ❏ Does everyone seem slower than you? (Yang)
- ❏ Is any kind of pressure a concern to you? (Yin)
- ❏ Do you thrive on pressure? (Yang)
- ❏ Are your fingernails thin and do they break easily? (Yin)
- ❏ Are your nails hard and thick? (Yang)
- ❏ Do you prefer darker colors and lighting? (Yin)
- ❏ Do you prefer brighter colors and lighting? (Yang)
- ❏ Are you often late? (Yin)
- ❏ Are you usually on time? (Yang)
- ❏ Are you a follower? (Yin)
- ❏ Are you a leader? (Yang)

the influence of lifestyle and livelihood

Our daily food and cooking styles are not the only two factors that determine our current condition. Our levels of physical activity, communication, intellectual activity, and recreational pursuits all have a bearing on whether our current condition is more yin or more yang.

Despite all strong physical activity being regarded as yang and any intellectual pursuit being broadly recognized as yin, there are very "yangizing" qualities that can be brought to bear regarding a livelihood that is largely centered around mental activity. For instance, "yangizing" versions of these tasks can be meeting deadlines, providing detailed data, discussing and generating new ideas with colleagues, selling, advertising, public relations, and management. Less taxing versions of yang physical activities include driving, security work, factory work, and night shifts.

On the following pages, I will outline four methods which can help you cope better with your livelihood through adjustments made in your cooking styles.

the "yangizing" effects of our livelihood include physical activity, social interaction, working in the material world, activities that are fast-paced, specific tasks, organizational roles, and any process involving gathering.

the "yinizing" effects of our livelihood include intellectual activities, working alone, spiritual practices, activities that are slow-paced, working with chi energy, planning, inventing, and working with the world of concepts.

These are cooking styles and ingredients that have the potential to bring warmth, strength, endurance, stamina, and an overall grounding effect.

"yangizing" meals

a "yangizing" meal

In northern Europe and northern Japan, the cold coastal waters provide the locals with an abundance of fresh herring. Being active and capable of withstanding the cold, these fish lean toward the yang end of the spectrum. In addition, their oily flesh provides a good source of B vitamins and their fine bones are rich in calcium and vitamin D. In these cold and dark climates where natural sunlight decreases the capacity to absorb vitamin D, the herring provided it instead. Early signs of a welfare state emerged in England during the fifteenth and sixteenth centuries when the poor of the parish were given a "dole" of herrings at least once a week.

While potatoes are rarely preferred to cereal grain by the Japanese, if cooked correctly they are a good source of starch which can aid stamina. Instinctively, the Japanese have come to terms with the yin nature of the potato and generally boil them together with small strips of kombu (a type of Japanese seaweed), to help leech out the higher content of potassium.

The length of time taken to prepare this dish has an overall "yangizing" effect and the ginger accentuates the warming quality.

traditional simmered
herring and potato

serves four

2 fresh herring fillets
8 small potatoes
1 4-inch strip of kombu seaweed
½ cup sake
¼ cup mirin
¼ cup soy sauce
1 teaspoon peeled freshly grated ginger
Sea salt to taste

step one: preparing the herring Wash the fishes in warm and moderately salty water and then remove the scales by scraping your knife from the tail toward the head. Gently remove each head by cutting just behind the pectoral fin, through the spine to the other side. Gut each fish by running the tip of the knife from the tail toward the head. Remove the guts, rinse the inside of the fish under cold water and then run the tip of the knife along either side of the spine from the tail toward the head to release any remaining blood in the cavity. Rinse again.

Next, working from the tail toward the head, begin to slice gently on either side of the spine. Take the knife to a depth of only half an inch and resist the temptation to try to "saw" into the fish. Light gentle strokes, slicing a little deeper each time toward the head, are best. Once about half an inch of the spine is exposed, lay the fish flat on your cutting board and make an incision just above the tail. With your blade facing the head, cut gently and continuously close to the spine. Use your free hand to lift the flesh away from the bone. Turn the fish over and repeat the process.

step two: cooking the potatoes Peel the potatoes and cut them into one-inch cubes. Bring them to the boil in a pan of water with a little salt and the strip of kombu for five minutes. Check them occasionally with a fork, as you only need to parboil them at this stage. Drain and set aside. Keep the strip of kombu for step three.

step three: cooking the herring Bring a small pan of water to a boil, with a pinch of salt and drop the herring fillets into the boiling water for half a minute. Remove them, run them under cold water, and dry them off with a towel.

Combine the sake, mirin, soy sauce, and kombu. Gently simmer the mixture in a saucepan with an additional cup of water. With their skins facing up, place the four fillets of herring into the saucepan and gently simmer for thirty minutes with the lid on. Remove the kombu, rinse it under fresh water, and cut it into four strips lengthwise. Add the parboiled potato cubes to the pan and continue to simmer for five or six more minutes, or until the potatoes are tender.

presentation Serve the dish hot in individual bowls garnishing each one with a strip of kombu and a pinch of grated ginger.

story

Finding the right balance of diet to support our lifestyle is often one of trial and error. I first became interested in Japanese macrobiotic cookery when I arrived in England in 1976, after spending the previous six years working my way round the world. In addition to preparing, cooking, and eating these strange new ingredients, I had taken up the Japanese martial art Aikido. This in turn led me to begin my studies in Shiatsu massage, a Japanese expression of acupressure which involves applying either palm or thumb pressure to the meridians of chi energy on the surface of the body.

To support myself as a student, I found a well paid job in the middle of the summer in the deep freeze compartment of a major ice cream company. My meals at this time were fairly simple and austere, consisting of plenty of rice, vegetables, salads, tofu, fruits, nuts, and seeds. I was not eating any animal food and had even decided to eliminate fish from my diet in the search of greater flexibility in my practice of Aikido. My companions at work, on the other hand, ate hearty breakfasts of bacon and eggs, had hot lunches, drank plenty of tea all day, and enjoyed hot meals of fish and chips or curries on their way home.

I froze in the deep freeze compared to them! After an hour in this environment, dressed to brave the Alaskan temperatures, we would have a break to warm up. I could not understand at the time why my companions recovered quickly from the fierce cold, whereas I spent my precious break time jumping up and down in the sunshine trying to defrost my toes. Eventually, my macrobiotic cooking instructor provided me with some simple advice. "You need more fire." Within days of introducing hot miso soup into my diet for breakfast, making the effort to drink fresh Japanese tea at work, and even bringing vegetable and bean-based stews to work in my thermos, I was able to withstand the extremes of the temperatures just as my companions did.

Even in extreme conditions such as this, where traditionally we may have eaten a more yang diet—higher in salt and animal products—we can increase the levels of yang in the cooking by increasing the amount of fire, time, pressure, and salt, without necessarily reverting to the use of animal foods. Of course it is an individual choice, but at least these four principles give us added flexibility as we endeavor to practice and understand the alchemy of cooking.

"yinizing" meals

Preparations and cooking styles that are calming, relaxing, and cooling, and bring us mental and physical flexibility.

a yin relaxing meal

Udon noodles are made from wheat and are regarded as more yin than their buckwheat (soba) counterparts. They have a mellow taste and texture. Tofu is a soya bean curd and is a rich source of calcium within the traditional Japanese diet. Tofu is made from soaked soya beans which are ground into a fine paste, brought to a boil in water for between five and eight minutes, and then separated into the pulp (unohana) and the milk itself. This liquid is then curdled with nigari, which is derived from sea salt. Once the curdling process begins, the mixture is placed in muslin-lined wooden or steel boxes and pressure is exerted for at least an hour to draw off the excess liquid and to firm up the tofu.

In its raw form, tofu is a very yin product. Of the principles of fire, pressure, time, and salt, tofu has only had pressure as a major force on it. Its cooling qualities are relaxing, and monks frequently ate raw tofu in their broths to put out the fire of any sexual desires they may have had. For the following dish, the tofu will be "yangized" through deep frying.

All mushrooms can be regarded as yin vegetables. They grow quickly at night and have a short shelf-life. However, the shiitake mushrooms grow slowly and retain their vitality. Usually they are dried for storage and then soaked for cooking. They have the added benefit of helping to dissolve excess fats and oils within our system. Again, like tofu, they have a cooling, more yin effect—but not excessively so.

noodles with tofu and mushroom broth

4 dried shiitake mushrooms

1 4-inch piece of kombu seaweed

2 onions

1 teaspoon of sea salt

14 ounces of udon noodles

3½ quarts of water

1 4-inch block of firm tofu

9 ounces plain flour, sieved

12 ounces ice-cold water

1 egg

sunflower oil for deep frying

soy sauce (shoyu) to taste

3 scallions

step one: preparing the broth Soak the mushrooms and the strip of kombu in separate dishes of cold water. Peel and halve the onions and cut them into very fine slices lengthwise. Sauté them gently with a pinch of salt in a deep pan until they appear translucent. Drain the mushrooms, remove their stalk bases, and finely slice. Add these to the pan with five serving bowls of water, a teaspoon of sea salt, and the strip of kombu and its soaking water. Bring up to the boil.

step two: cooking udon noodles Udon noodles are best cooked in a deep saucepan with plenty of water. Bring at least three and a half quarts of water to a boil. Make sure that there is a depth of two to three inches free at the top of the saucepan. As the cooking time varies from different producers, check the cooking time on the packet. "Shock" the udon at least twice by pouring in about one cup of cold water as they come to a rapid boil. Let them simmer gently for the final few minutes.

step three: cooking the tofu Wash the block of tofu under running water and pat it dry with a cloth. Cut the block into half-inch cubes. Prepare a batter mix with the flour, ice-cold water, and egg as outlined on page 136. Pour sunflower oil into a heavy cast-iron pot to a depth of at least three inches and heat to approximately 360° F. Deep-fry the tofu as explained on page 136.

presentation Once the udon noodles are cooked, rinse them immediately under cold, running water and place a quantity in each of the four bowls. In the last few minutes of cooking, season the broth with soy sauce, according to taste. Place the deep-fried tofu on top of the noodles, and pour the broth through a sieve into the bowls. Garnish each bowl with finely chopped, diagonally sliced sections of scallion. Serve piping hot with chopsticks.

cooking brown rice

When cooked correctly, brown rice is a delicious grain and can be a meal in itself. Cooked in too much water, or for too long or too short a time, brown rice can be quite unappetizing. Unlike meat, which loses its essence the longer you chew it, brown rice tastes more delicious by the mouthful. Also the bigger the volume of rice you prepare, the more delicious it is. Since brown rice retains its chi for several days and since the preparation time is quite lengthy (up to forty minutes), it is worth considering cooking more than you need and then re-heating it in a stir-fry or simply by steaming it.

pressure-cooked brown rice Wash two cups of rice in cold running water in a sieve to remove any dust or debris. Wash the rice again, this time in a large bowl, and allow any husks or other floating debris to overflow. Put the brown rice in a pan and add three cups of spring water. Add a quarter of a teaspoon of good quality sea salt. Close the pressure cooker and bring the unit up to pressure, reduce the heat and allow it to simmer gently for forty minutes. To reduce the possibility of scorching the rice at the base of the pot, place a steel flame deflector under the pressure cooker.

After forty minutes, remove the pot from the flame and allow the pressure to reduce at its own pace. Do not be tempted to place the pressure cooker under cold running water in an effort to speed up the process. Gently remove the lid and stir the contents with a wooden spatula or Japanese bamboo rice paddle.

boiled brown rice Wash two cups of rice under cold running water, and then again in a bowl to allow any debris or chaff to overflow. In a heavy cast-iron pot with a well-fitting lid, combine the brown rice with four cups of spring water and a quarter of a teaspoon of good quality sea salt.

Bring the ingredients to a rapid boil without the lid. Once the ingredients are boiling, cover and reduce the flame slightly so that the rice is still visibly boiling. Keep it at this temperature for twenty minutes.

For the final thirty minutes of cooking, reduce the flame to a low simmer and slip a steel, heat-deflecting pad between the pot and the flame.

Just before removing the pot from the flame, slide out the heat deflector and give the pot a burst of high flame for one minute. Turn off the flame, move the pot to a cooler location, and let it sit for five minutes. Stir the ingredients and let them settle for a further five minutes before serving or using the rice for the sauté dish that follows.

spiritual meals

Not only to support spiritual practices, but to clarify and sharpen your mental agility. By removing the extreme and scattered qualities of sugar and refined food, the chi of the cooking and the ingredients combine to bring clear vision.

a meal for clear thinking or spiritual practices

Rice has been cultivated throughout the Middle East, the Indian subcontinent, China, and the rest of the Far East for centuries. Refined or polished rice was only used in times of celebration, or as a staple within the ruling classes of China and Japan. With the advent of the rice-milling machine in the latter part of the nineteenth century, refined white rice became a staple.

Despite its richness of vitamins and minerals, whole-grain brown rice is often regarded in the Far East now as a reminder of hard times, poverty, and sickness. In Japan it was quite common for grandmothers to insist that you eat brown rice if you felt sick, hence its association with illness.

Arame is a dark, dried, wiry sea vegetable, rich in minerals and with many trace elements. It always needs washing and soaking before cooking and has long been associated in Japan with its capacity to cleanse the blood. For centuries, the Japanese turned their backs on any source of animal food except fish, and their rich reserves of sea vegetables provided them with the minerals that soup stock made from animal bones would have provided in former times and in the West.

Tofu, with its gentle yin cooling quality, helps to calm the mind and the soul and encourages clarity. The gentle cooking style of sauté is another calming and settling influence that the following recipe provides.

stir-fried brown rice
and vegetables

serves four

1 cup of sesame seeds
$\frac{1}{10}$ ounce of dry arame sea vegetable
2 onions
Sesame oil
Pinch of sea salt or 1 teaspoon soy sauce (shoyu)
2 medium carrots
2 cups of organic, short-grain, brown rice
Nori seaweed or finely chopped parsley to garnish

step one: roasting the sesame seeds Wash the sesame seeds in a fine steel strainer under running water. Put a heavy, cast-iron pan or skillet onto a medium flame and empty the sesame seeds into the pan. Continue to stir the sesame seeds until they turn golden brown and a few of them begin to pop and crackle. Remove them and allow to cool in an open bowl.

step two: preparing the vegetables Wash the arame seaweed under running water and then place it in a bowl, cover it with a little water, and allow it to soak for five to six minutes. Peel and dice the onions into ⅛-inch cubes. Wash and finely slice the carrots diagonally, and slice them again lengthwise into matchsticks.

step three: stir-frying brown rice and vegetables Cover the surface of a heavy cast-iron skillet with good quality, cold-pressed sesame oil. Turn up the heat a bit and sauté the onion with a pinch of sea salt or soya sauce until it is translucent. Add the carrot and continue to stir. Remove the arame from the water and squeeze out any excess liquid. Toss it in with the onion and carrot and stir them together for two minutes.

Slowly add the prepared brown rice *(see pages 178–179)* to the pan and stir gently to prevent the mixture from sticking or scorching. If you feel that the dish needs a little more liquid, add the water you used for soaking the arame, which is now rich in minerals that have been leached off. Continue stirring until the rice is hot enough. Add a little soy sauce to taste during the final one or two minutes and mix in the sesame seeds.

presentation Serve the stir-fry in bowls, which helps to preserve the heat of the dish while you chew it slowly and quietly. Garnish with quarter-inch strips of nori seaweed or finely chopped parsley.

social meals

If you want or need to interact with others, share concepts and feelings, then a meal needs to have plenty of variety, richness, and even a little spice. The purpose of this approach to cooking is to bring people together and to allow their chi to express itself.

a social meal

One-pot cooking is an exciting way of bringing friends or colleagues together to share a meal. The autumn and the winter months are best for a style of cooking called *nabe*. A nabe pot can be made of cast iron, but traditionally an earthenware casserole pot with a lid is used. Most of the ingredients are parboiled by the host in advance, and then the nabe pot is placed at the center of the table with a cooking source, such as a small burner, underneath. The ingredients to be dipped in the pot are displayed on the table around this central feature. A variety of condiments and sauces are also provided to suit the different guests' tastes. In addition to the main meal, Westerners may like a little extra food on the side, such as a few bowls of cooked rice or noodles. The gently flavored chicken stew is boosted by the pungent sauce made from a mixture of lemon and lime juice and soy sauce known in Japan as ponzu.

Huddled together sharing this meal—but at the same time choosing what you would like to dip in the pot and how long to cook it for—makes for a rewarding and memorable experience. If you accompany the meal with earthenware cups of warm sake, conversation, ideas, and the warmth of friendship will soon begin to flow.

one-pot chicken (tori-mizutaki)

serves six

ponzu sauce

6 tablespoons soy sauce *(shoyu)*

4 tablespoons lemon juice

2 tablespoons lime juice

1 tablespoon mirin

1 tablespoon rice vinegar

1 4-inch strip of kombu seaweed

nabe

8 pints of water

1 4-inch strip of kombu seaweed

1 teaspoon of sea salt

3 whole chicken breasts,
   diced into 1-inch cubes

4 pints fresh chicken stock

2 pounds Chinese cabbage

4 large carrots *(cut into flower
   shapes as described on page 244)*

½ pound fresh firm tofu,
   cut into 1-inch cubes

6 dried or fresh shiitake mushrooms

12 small white button mushrooms

1 bunch of watercress

6 scallions

condiments

½ cup roasted sesame seeds

4 fresh scallions

½ teaspoon fresh raw root ginger

1 2-inch piece of raw daikon,
   finely grated

shoyu *(soy sauce)*

step one: preparing the ponzu sauce To get the most from this delicious sauce, it is wise to prepare the ingredients the day before and let them mature overnight in a glass container in the cold.

Simply mix the soy sauce together with the lemon and lime juices, mirin, and rice vinegar. I prefer to use brown rice vinegar. Rinse the strip of kombu under the tap to remove any excess salt and place that in the mixture.

step two: preparing the ingredients for the nabe In a saucepan, put eight pints of water, a teaspoon of sea salt, and the strip of kombu and bring to a rapid boil. Drop in the chicken pieces and parboil them for ten minutes. Remove them from the broth and dash them under cold running water to arrest the cooking process. Add the fresh chicken stock to the remaining water and the kombu and let this simmer gently.

Take the Chinese cabbage and remove the base along with the harder, lower section of the white stem. Separate the leaves, and drop them into slightly salty boiling water for two minutes. Remove them quickly, run them under cold water, and put them aside to cool. Place five or six cooked leaves in layers at one end of a Japanese bamboo mat (sundare) which is used when making sushi. Tightly roll the leaves to squeeze out any excess water and then unroll the sundare. Trim off the ends of the roll and slice the main portion into one-inch rings. Arrange these carefully in a separate dish for the table.

Trim the bottoms and tops of the carrots. Chop them into two to three-inch lengths. Cut ⅛-inch grooves at five equidistant points around the carrot. Slice them as thinly as you can (⅛ inch or less), and parboil them in water (without salt) for one minute. Run them under cold water and arrange them in a separate dish.

Cut the firm fresh tofu into 1-inch cubes and display them in a dish. If you are using dried shiitake mushrooms, they will need soaking for at least twenty minutes before preparation. Once they are soaked you can follow the same preparation method as with fresh shiitake mushrooms. Remove two-thirds of the stalk and cut a deep cross into the top of each mushroom. Parboil these for ten minutes.

Wash and drain the button mushrooms, then remove the lower part of their stalks and present them in their own bowl. Wash, clean, and separate out the bunch of fresh watercress so that you have at least twelve healthy sprigs to display on one dish. Wash and trim the six scallions and display them on a dish.

step three: preparing the condiments Have available at the table, close enough for all the guests to reach, a variety of small dishes containing the following condiments:

- freshly roasted sesame seeds
- finely chopped scallions
- peeled raw root ginger that has been grated finely
- finely grated daikon
- soy sauce *(shoyu)*

presentation Begin by sieving the contents of the pot in which you prepared the chicken, removing the kombu and any remaining pieces of chicken or skin. Bring this stock up to the boil and place it in your earthenware pot or nabe pot at the center of the table with a source of heat underneath. Surround the central pot with all the ingredients and the optional side dishes of noodles or rice.

Everyone can then join in by dipping the ingredients into the pot and cooking them how they wish, and completing the process using ponzu dipping sauce or any of the condiments provided.

afterthought It is traditional to complete the meal by sharing small bowls of the remaining broth. It has all the richness of a chicken broth along with the vital minerals and tastes from the vegetables that have been prepared in it.

story

The amount of liquid we consume every day plays an important role in balancing our condition toward more yin or more yang. In a temperate climate our bodies need between three and six quarts of fluid a day to compensate for the loss of fluid through urination, perspiration, and breathing. But this does not mean that we actually have to drink this amount of fluid, as vegetables, salad, and fruit contain up to 90 percent liquid. Other sources are soups, stews, and, of course, drinks themselves. To remain fit and healthy we do need this minimum three quarts a day to compensate for this natural loss. However, the current fashion for drinking in excess of this, while not harming the kidneys, does not in any way benefit the elimination process. In fact, it can make it work a lot harder.

In 1972, while working in the desert of the Northern Territory in Australia, we were encouraged to consume gallons of fluid a day, accompanied by additional salt tablets. Working with a heavy jack hammer under the sun where temperatures were 104° F in the shade, it was very tempting to follow the advice of the foreman. However, I found that the more I drank the more I sweated and the more I needed, or felt I needed, to replenish the fluid. Apart from the physical work, my main memories of these gruelling days involved sweating and drinking, and sweating and drinking!

Several weeks later I had the opportunity to work alongside an older, local Aborigine laborer. I could not help noticing how little he sweated and how seldom he went to the water cooler. He quietly got on with his work, operating at the same level that I was. Over a break one day, I asked him why he did not sweat so much. He simply replied, "I do not drink very much."

In 1974, while crossing the Sahara Desert in the back of a truck accompanied by 40 Tauregs and many of their goats, I was again quietly surprised how little water they each took in preparation for this four-day journey. As we approached the southern, hotter end of the Sahara, the area was in the grip of one of the worst heatwaves and droughts in living memory. Carcasses of cattle, goats, and camels lay everywhere, and there were many dehydrated mothers and children visible by the roadside as we came closer to civilization.

On one occasion, deep in the desert, during a sandstorm when the truck was barely able to move faster than walking pace because of the wind, a towering figure loomed out of the gloom. He was a lone Tuareg accompanied only by his camel. He gracefully asked the driver to stop. Wizened, with skin as hard as leather, he held up a calabash and asked for water. The driver filled up the bowl with some four quarts of precious water. I will never forget how he simply dipped his hand in, took one mouthful, and then gave the rest to the camel, waved us goodbye, and wandered off into the desert. He had conditioned himself to be so yang that he could survive in these harsh conditions without any fear of real dehydration. Had it been me, I would have abandoned the camel, jumped on the truck, and asked to be taken to the nearest watering hole!

story

Our bodies, including our circulatory and digestive systems, are wonderful, self-balancing systems. We never consciously ask our lungs to breathe or our hearts to beat, or request that our livers pull their weight to compensate for a heavy, late-night meal. But we can make the job easier if we are a little more conscious of what we eat and how we prepare it to match our condition. Sometimes, however, we can allow our thoughts and our deeds to get in the way. I have made this mistake many times myself.

In the run up to Christmas 1980, I had a very busy schedule. As Christmas vacation approached, I was really looking forward to a period of "yinization", chilling out, relaxing, and being with my family. In the back of my mind I was also conscious that the following day I had a flight booked to Boston for a week-long teacher training seminar which would culminate in a practical and theoretical examination of my cooking and diagnostic skills. After a day of relaxation on Christmas Eve, I felt all the symptoms of a cold coming on. Intuitively, I felt that this was a release and a way of letting go of tension and that I should ride it out. But then the logic of "doing" said that I was becoming yin, that within two days I would be under pressure (yang) that I would have a week of studies (yang) and an examination (yang) and that I had better get myself yang and into shape pretty quickly. I succeeded in suppressing all the symptoms of the cold quite quickly by reducing my fluid intake, having plenty of salty miso soup, using plenty of Japanese pickles with my meals, and avoiding anything that even looked, smelled, or tasted of yin!

The trip went well, the studies were a challenge and involved full days from dawn until late. The final few hours before departing for London involved the rigorous exam. While still in yang mode I returned to London, traveled across town in the early morning rush hour ("yangizing"), opened the door to my home, and from my yang perspective thought my wife and young son looked too yin! I said as much and soon found myself back on the underground and behind my desk while many of my colleagues were drifting in from their Christmas break. Oblivious to the fact that I was too tight, too wired—too yang—I set about doing the bookkeeping for the institute which was something I found challenging, detailed, and "yangizing."

A colleague of mine who had enjoyed the Christmas break wandered past my desk, and in that moment I knew he was quietly assessing my condition. Politely, yet firmly, he insisted that I go home, take a hot bath, and go to bed. In addition, he suggested that I put a drop or two of whisky in a fresh cup of tea with some lemon and sweet barley malt.

I went home, had at least two hot toddies and by midday I was well into a sweat, curled up in bed, releasing all the yang and the tension that I had artificially imposed on myself to get through this difficult phase. This is a good example of how, when we allow our condition to become too extreme—whether this be more yin or more yang—we cannot see the other end of the spectrum, or even begin to adjust our lifestyle or cooking accordingly. It is at these extreme ends of the spectrum that we usually hit a wall and, painful though it can be from time to time, at least it sets us on the course of regaining balance and finding our center again.

chapter 5

presentation

meditation: The truth of Zen, just a bit of it, is what turns one's humdrum life, a life of monotonous, uninspiring commonplaces, into one of art, full of genuine inner creativity.

—D. T. Suzuki

In Zen cooking, the final presentation of the meal is like a signature from the chef. It is the chef's way of signing off, of wishing you good health, and giving you a short moment for contemplation. On a sensory level, the visual impact of the meal acts as an appetizer. Given that the portions of food traditionally served in a Japanese monastery, or even a Japanese restaurant, are relatively small, a high degree of satisfaction is achieved by the sight and presentation of the meal.

attention to detail

From the understanding that we are all unique, comes the understanding that our daily foods, our cooking styles, and indeed our volume of consumption, need subtle adjustment for each person. Rather than preparing a wide range of different dishes, the main meal can be adjusted simply by using a variety of sauces, dips, or condiments.

Certain foods and cooking styles, while delicious and appetizing, can sometimes tax our digestive system. Examples of this include oily dishes such as tempura, seafood, and animal products. The secret to making these ingredients more digestible is to provide small amounts of an appropriate balancing agent. Good quality vinegar, soy sauce, daikon, or ginger can make all the difference by neutralising any potential discomfort caused by the cooking style or ingredient. This is a very true understanding of the Zen principle of Right Attention. Rather than experiencing indigestion and reaching for an alkalising agent in a tablet, it is wiser to build a preventive element into the meal in the first place.

the five elements and their tastes

Central to Zen cookery are the choices one makes about cooking styles and ingredients as well as the application of the Chinese five-element theory. Each of the five elements (Water, Wood, Fire, Earth, Metal) can have a corresponding season, time of day, internal organ, shape, emotion, taste, and color. Since the essence of Zen cookery is to create balance, it is important to pay attention to the final presentation of the meal in terms of garnishes, proportions, and accompanying dips and sauces.

When considering the kinds of seasonings to use with a meal, or the flavor of a sauce or garnish, the following five tastes are associated with the elements.

Water is the chi of winter, night time, and dormancy. It is a phase of energy which invokes the spirit of resting, recharging, and hibernating. Although on the surface this phase may appear still and dark, its deeper essence is strong and powerful.

Taste–salty	*miso, soy sauce, salt*

Wood epitomizes the spirit of spring, dawn and new growth, freshness, vitality, and youth. In the *I Ching* this phase is mirrored in the natural world as thunder.

Taste–sour	*good quality vinegars, sharp-tasting pickles*

Fire transforms when chi energy is at its peak. This is represented by the summer season and midday. It is an active phase and the one when we feel the most charged and enlightened. Fire's tendency is to grow upwards and outwards.

Taste–bitter	roasted seeds, roasted seaweed, bitter greens, olives.

Earth is associated with late summer and the afternoon, when chi energy begins to settle and gather. It is a mellow phase which brings with it a sense of richness and nurturing—Earth is really representative here of soil and compost.

Taste–sweet	dried fruits, corn, chestnuts, pumpkin

Metal is the most gathering and "yangizing" of all the phases. It represents the time of harvest—the autumn—and the time of day when we return from work and focus on our lives and families—the evening. It has concentrated, dense chi with the potential to endure difficulties and hardship.

Taste–spicy/pungent	scallion tops, daikon, ginger, mustard

the five colors

Integrating a variety of colors to represent the elements will create a sense of balance and harmony. Proportionally they do not need to be equal. Just a subtle addition of any one of these colors to the meal can make a difference. Examples include:

water— black or purple: arame seaweed, burdock root

wood— green: spring greens, broccoli

fire— red or pink: radish, red pepper

earth— yellow or orange: pumpkin, corn

metal— white: scallion root, daikon

the five shapes

Grains, beans, tofu, fish, and meat do not fit into well-defined shapes from a five-element perspective, however, vegetables do. Different vegetables subtly reveal different aspects of the five elements, as the following examples indicate:

water—Downward growth: root vegetables

wood—Straight upward growth: leeks, scallions, chives

fire— Tall outward growth: Chinese cabbage, chard

earth—Round: pumpkin, onion, cabbage

metal—Condensed: watercress, sea vegetables

Broadly speaking, all vegetables could be regarded as part of the Wood phase when you compare them to fish (Water), poultry (Fire), grains (Earth), and seeds and condiments (Metal).

story

My favorite staple food when I am traveling is the rice ball. Traditionally made and used by monks in Japanese temples, the humble rice ball is a meal in itself. Chewed peacefully and slowly, it is satisfying food, and by correctly combining ingredients and style of preparation it will represent all the five phases in one product.

Rice balls reflect all phases in the cycle of the five elements. To begin with, grains can be regarded as Earth energy, the most condensed of which are brown rice, which represents Metal. The process of pressure cooking is also Metal. The umeboshi plum is sour in taste and represents Wood. The sheets of nori seaweed have a combination of the floating energy of Water and the bitter taste of Fire. The sun-drying process that cures the nori, also represents Fire.

Rice balls are easy to prepare and can keep two to three days, retaining their chi and moisture. On a long flight, when you have plenty of time to chew well, they are much better than the in-flight meal. On one flight to the United States, the Japanese passenger sitting next to me was fascinated with my rice ball and could not resist asking me what I was eating. When I explained and showed him the ingredients, he asked if I was sick! He associated traditional products, such as brown rice and umeboshi with stories his grandparents had told him of difficult times. From his point of view people only eat brown rice if they are either poor or trying to regain their health by returning to simple unpolished rice.

A meal consisting of two or three rice balls and a bottle of spring water is quite sufficient to sustain you through a long flight, provided you chew each mouthful between 50 and 100 times. Airline travel can be a disorientating experience, and the food offered will lack any strong chi as it will inevitably have been prepared a day earlier and then reheated on board.

rice balls

for four rice balls

2 cups short-grain brown rice
2 sheets of nori seaweed
1 umeboshi plum

step one: making the rice ball Begin by making a pot of pressure-cooked, short-grain brown rice *(see page 178)*. Wait for the rice to cool to room temperature before transferring it to a lightly oiled wooden bowl. With moist hands, take a handful of rice and press it firmly between your cupped hands to form a ball. The harder you press, the firmer the rice becomes and the more yang chi you will give it, helping it to last longer.

step two: preparing the nori Take a sheet of nori seaweed *(available from most natural food shops)* and lightly toast it on both sides over a flame. If you have an electric cooker you could use a candle. Cut the sheet of nori into quarters. Wrap one of the quarters around half of the rice ball pressing firmly as you do so and lightly dabbing the corners of the nori sheet with water if it is not sticking to the rice.

step three: adding the umeboshi plum (*It is preferable to buy the plums from a natural food shop.*) Using the tip of a wooden chopstick, poke a hole into the exposed half of the rice ball. Pinch off approximately a quarter of the flesh of a umeboshi plum, and using the chopstick, place it in the center of the rice ball. Once the piece of umeboshi is buried in the center of the ball, squeeze the rice ball together and cover the exposed part of the rice ball with another quarter sheet of nori, dabbing down any loose edges with a little water.

providing the spark

Applying the principles of Zen cooking to your daily diet need not result in you eating monastic food. Although traditionally food that supported spiritual practices needed to be simple and sustaining, there are creative ways that we can all harness the energy of "stronger" foods. These stronger foods could be regarded as extreme from a yin/yang point of view. They include rich or oily foods, seafood, fish, eggs, meat, and even sugar. A simple diet of grains, vegetables, tofu, soups, and fruit—foods without any real "spark"—can be a dulling and uninspiring experience. The condiments, the side dishes, the colors, the tastes, and the variety of textures can all provide the spark.

Part of the yin/yang approach to cooking lies in the skill of being able to transform any raw material in the kitchen and gain sustenance from it. Strong foods, such as salmon, or challenging styles of cooking, such as tempura, can have the vital energy needed to provide a spark if we understand how to balance and prepare them.

When I first began to integrate Zen cookery into my life in the 1970s when I was living in London, I felt a deep sense of peace and security. However, on reflection, my diet was bland. I lacked that spark of creativity and humor that I recalled from a few years earlier in my travels around the world. Despite the fact that I found new levels of energy and contentment in my life and was quite happy with my monastic diet, every few weeks I found myself in a fish and chip shop! The rich, oily, crisp fish and chips, covered with plenty of salt and vinegar, were just what I needed! When I talked to other colleagues I discovered that they also found themselves from time to time attracted to chocolate, coffee, toast and butter, beer, gateau, ice cream, bacon and eggs, or scrambled eggs on toast. Why were we all doing this and what was missing? Clearly, each one of those foods was giving us something that we were missing. If we are craving something sour or salty or sweet or rich, then it is obvious that this is missing from our diet. Once I began to integrate some of these flavors into my diet, the cravings began to dissolve.

If you find yourself in a similar
situation in the future, begin by reflecting on what you
have been eating during the past ten days and adjust your cooking
style accordingly. If, despite this approach you would still like to experiment with
foods that have extreme chi and do not wish to be knocked completely off balance, the
following guidelines may be helpful:

- **go for the best quality possible** If you fancy a piece of chocolate gateau, then go to the best
patisserie in town and choose the finest example of their product.

- **share the experience with someone else** Eating alone in this situation can often leave you feeling
guilty or self-indulgent. Bring a friend, and enjoy the occasion together in a light-hearted mood. Your
companion will also make sure (you hope) that you will not eat three or four slices.

- **have no more than two helpings** It has been my experience that one and sometimes two portions
of a so-called extreme food is what your body actually needs at that time to redress the balance.
It is rather like a cold drink on a hot day—one glass, perhaps two, does the job very well, but
the third will leave you feeling bloated or uncomfortable.

- **chew well** Thist will be covered fully in the next chapter.

story

In London during the economic boom of the 1980s new coffee shops with luxurious interiors began to sprout in the basements of many of the new, big businesses. A couple of times a week, when the pressure of work was high, colleagues and I would meet at 7AM for a breakfast meeting. One morning a group of Japanese businessmen arrived and seated themselves toward the back of the restaurant. The man who was clearly the boss sat with his back to the wall facing the entrance.

While the men around him snacked on toast, croissant, Danish pastry, and tea, the boss tucked into scrambled eggs and smoked salmon. Salmon itself is an extremely powerful fish, its chi is rich in stamina, endurance, and focus. How else could this fish travel thousands of miles across the ocean and return to the river of its birth? When we eat salmon, especially the more yang versions (smoked), we can absorb its chi and character—determined, single-minded, and focused. Imagine starting off your day with this invigorating kind of fuel compared to the dull and dissipating effect of croissants and pastries.

Add to the salmon a couple of scrambled eggs and you are really getting down to business! Eggs are the most condensed (yang) of all foods available to us. At least by scrambling them and making them more fluffy and adding a garnish of chives or scallions, we can offset the potential rigidity that they can provide.

the right balance

For centuries in the West we have found ways to balance our foods by using condiments, side dishes and sauces. For example, the Sunday roast beef is traditionally served with horseradish (Metal/pungent); ham is served with pineapple (Earth/sweet); smoked salmon with lemon (Wood/sour); steak with pepper or mustard (Metal/pungent); roast pork with apple sauce (Earth/sweet). Oysters and tomato juice are both yin, cold products dominated by the Water element–a favorite accompaniment to them is tabasco, which is spicy and pungent (Metal). Smoked salmon and caviar are both extremely yang foods and are usually accompanied by wedges of lemon (Wood energy) or champagne (Wood/Fire energy). Any meat product can benefit from being prepared with mushrooms or barley. A Stroganoff is rich in mushrooms, and traditional nineteenth-century stews always had a handful of barley present. Finely minced scallions as a garnish on any meat dish is helpful. Eggs, given that they have a very contracting yang nature, are best made more mellow by including mushrooms as a side dish, garnished with chives or parsley. The most primitive form of animal life can be classified as shellfish. Most are absolutely delicious, but it only takes one small portion to leave you feeling extremely ill. Always eat them with a small side dish of raw, grated daikon and a squeeze of lemon. Any preparation of cooked fish will benefit from a garnish of either parsley, lemon, finely minced scallions, or grated raw root daikon. Good quality vinegar is also beneficial.

"Try not to achieve

anything special."

condi-ments

When you cook for other people, whether it be for your family or catering for a larger group, it is best to season the food lightly while you cook and allow individuals at the table to adjust it according to their needs. This is important when you consider young children at the table as their salt requirement is less than that of an adult. By having a selection of condiments on hand, each individual can balance their own meal with small amounts of this concentrated form of yang food. These concentrated minerals can be likened to the value and power of gold and diamonds. We use neither in excess, however owning even a small quantity is a symbol of yang chi–persevering, durable, a sign of commitment, clarity, weight, and power.

gomashio

The name of this condiment is derived from goma, meaning sesame seeds, and shio, which is salt. Salt is a vital mineral to us all, but it is best ingested in the small and large intestine. When we cook with salt it penetrates the food and its essence is released deep down in the digestive system. When we eat salt raw—as a condiment at the table or, for example, sprinkled on roasted nuts—the salt is absorbed in the mouth and stomach. The absorption process is quite violent and quick, relative to the slow, mellow release of cooked salt in the small and large intestine. The quick absorption can result in an immediate desire for more fluid or sweet foods.

Gomashio cleverly takes this into consideration. It is made of washed, roasted, and semi-ground sesame seeds and lightly roasted, good-quality sea salt in proportions varying between 7:1 and 21:1. When these two substances are ground together, the salt attaches itself to the oil of the sesame seeds and is released slowly in the lower part of the digestive system. It tastes mildly salty and has a delicious, nutty flavor. I highly recommend using a teaspoon of gomaschio on any grain dish. It is even delicious sprinkled on porridge in the morning.

It is possible to buy the product in a good natural food store, but making gomashio yourself at home is a relaxing and meditative process. Individuals who are more yang would prefer a 7:1 ratio; a more yin variety, which is better suited for the elderly and young children is 20:1. For everyday adult use, I would recommend 14:1.

gomashio

2 cups raw, unhulled seeds
1½ - 4½ tablespoons sea salt (see previous page)

step one: preparing the sesame seeds Begin by washing approximately two cups of sesame seeds in a fine steel mesh. Drain away as much excess water as possible, and slowly roast them in a heavy, cast-iron skillet, continually stirring them with a wooden spatula until they are golden brown and begin to pop. Avoid using a high flame as they will burn and leave a bitter taste. The seeds are ready for crushing together with the salt when you can easily crush a sesame seed between the thumb and the tip of your little finger.

When the seeds are ready, place them in a surabachi—a Japanese ceramic mortar with a serrated interior. Allow them to cool slightly while you roast the sea salt.

step two: preparing the salt Continuously stir the sea salt on a low flame until you smell the chlorine coming off and the salt turns a slightly rusty color. Add the salt to the roasted sesame seeds and gently grind them together with the wooden pestle.

step three: making the gomashio   Keep the wooden pestle vertical, holding it gently in your right hand in much the same way that you would hold a calligraphy brush. Gently rest the palm of your left hand on top of the pestle and rotate the base of the pestle in a clockwise motion from the outside of the bowl towards the center. From the center, rotate counter-clockwise out toward the edges. Keep repeating this until 80 percent of the seeds are crushed. You can now store this condiment in a jar for up to three weeks.

afterthought   For headaches and tiredness resulting from eating sugar, try placing a teaspoon of gomaschio at the bottom of a teacup and pour boiling hot kukicha tea over the top. Stir it well and drink hot. Kukicha is part of the same tea plant that green tea is derived from. Kukicha literally means twig tea. The more mature and drier twigs of the bush are harvested after three years and dried. A small handful of twigs can be boiled in three cups of water for ten to fifteen minutes to form a refreshing, slightly alkaline drink. Regarded as the tea of the poor, it is rich in calciumand and unlike green tea has no tannin and caffeine.

tekka

This is one condiment that I would not recommend making at home in a hurry. I tried it once, and it cost me four hours of time and the ruin of one of my favorite cast-iron pans. Tekka is a Japanese condiment which combines the word tetsu, meaning iron, with ka, meaning fire.

The condiment is extremely yang and concentrated, and involves four hours of continuous stirring as you sauté the burdock, carrots, lotus root, ginger, and miso in a small amount of sesame oil. Years ago, it would take 16 hours to make!

As far as root vegetables are concerned, burdock and lotus root are the most yang. Wild burdock is often no thicker than a pencil, yet drives itself up to two feet into the ground. Burdock is used in many Japanese recipes and forms the basis of many winter stews. Its strength lies in supporting the chi of the kidneys and adrenal glands which recharge themselves in the winter when the burdock is at its strongest. In 1979, I grew rows of cultivated burdock and dandelion on my allotment and to my surprise was called up in front of the allotment committee one Sunday morning for growing "weeds" on my plot!

Lotus root in its fresh form has very powerful yang chi. It sits in the mud and silt at the bottom of ponds and draws up nutrients through its roots, and long stem, to the open leaf and flower floating on the surface of the pond. It is an especially useful supplement for strengthening the lungs and colon.

Tekka can be bought in natural food stores and needs to be used sparingly. It has a bitter and salty flavor with a crumbly texture. Use no more than an eighth to a quarter of a teaspoon sprinkled on cooked grains on alternate days.

A quarter of a teaspoon of tekka on top of softly cooked brown rice is an excellent remedy for diarrhea.

umeboshi plum

Far from being sweet as you might expect from a plum, these small, pink, shriveled, unripe, Japanese apricots are surprisingly sour and salty!

Umeboshi plums are a fine example of how the Japanese, as an island race, have made use of and appreciated every aspect of their local flora. It is hard to believe that they found great medicinal value in this tiny fruit that never ripened or matured fully, but fell from the trees sour and unripe in the early spring. The dew and consequent frost would continue to make them shrivel and look even more unappetizing.

Harvested in the early spring, dried in the weak sun of spring and further "yangized" by the frost, these small fruits are layered in barrels of sea salt, wrapped in shiso leaves. By applying pressure and time (both yang factors) the familiar pink umeboshi plums are ready some eighteen months later.

A jar of these plums will keep for years in the refrigerator, and they are rich in minerals—particularly phosphorous, iron, and calcium. They have a strong alkalizing effect and help us to maintain the mild alkaline pH of our blood. They have a mild antiseptic property and a small portion of plum held in your mouth can be useful in combating acute toothaches or dealing with mouth ulcers.

Umeboshi plums are an excellent remedy for diarrhea, for headaches and to neutralize (alkalize) our blood when it has become too acid due to the consumption of sugar, fat, and refined flour products. I also highly recommend them in your travel kit to help prevent any digestive disorders from drinking poor quality water.

Keep these plums on your table as a condiment and eat them at the end of a meal. A quarter or half a plum is quite adequate. They can be bought in paste form (use a quarter to half a teaspoon) or as whole plums. The whole plums also contain the stone, and it is worth keeping these in the jar for times when you have toothache or an acid stomach. Simply suck on the stone for several hours.

story

I love boats and sailing, but one of the worst afflictions to have at sea is motion sickness. Sometimes I get it, sometimes I do not. I tried using a small portion of umeboshi and found it helped prevent the onset of seasickness. One of my Japanese teachers recommended an even better remedy: to place a whole umeboshi plum in my navel and hold it there with a Band-Aid! How on earth would this work? From a yin/yang perspective, our balance could be seen to emanate from our hara rather than from our inner ear. If our hara is out of balance–yin–then we need to bring some strong yang to the center. I could see the logic of the plum in my navel, and indeed tried it— it worked!

In 1982 I took thirty students from the Kushi Institute in London on a ferry to Holland to spend a few days studying with their Dutch colleagues at the Kushi Institute in Amsterdam. It was an opportunity to study together, party together, and play basketball to let off steam. The overnight trip from Harwich to Holland in November was particularly rough and many of the students were violently sick. On the way back one of the wilder, more gregarious students, John, asked what he could do to prevent seasickness on the way home so that he could enjoy partying on the ship. I told him the anecdote of the umeboshi held in the navel by a Band-Aid.

As we disembarked early on the following morning after another fairly rough crossing, a dishevelled-looking John appeared saying that he had had a wonderful time, had not slept at all, had danced the night away, and it really had worked! At customs, we lost sight of John.

Later I learned that customs officers did not like the look of John, so they searched his bag and then searched him. What kind of an answer could he give them to the strange pickled, shriveled object taped into his navel! He told them it was an umeboshi plum and had to sit patiently for five hours while it was sent to a laboratory to be verified.

nori
seaweed

For centuries the vast range of sea vegetables growing in the coastal waters around Japan have provided its inhabitants with a valuable source of minerals and trace elements.

In much the same way that in the West we have drawn our source from the marrow and bones of animal foods, the Japanese took to the sea. Other colder shores, such as those around Maine, Ireland, Great Britain, Brittany and Scandinavia, all have a similar resource that those people have tapped into in the past. During the horrendous potato famine in Ireland, for example, many survivors in the north-western province of Sligo owed their survival to the nutrients provided by sea vegetables.

Botanically known as porphyra tenera, nori is harvested and boiled down into a sticky mass. It is then spread out to dry on large wooden frames in the sunshine and air. Paper thin, these sheets are cut into standard eight x six inch sheets, and are available, hermetically sealed, from any natural food store. I would encourage you to purchase nori at one of these shops rather than at a Japanese food emporium, which tends to preserve the product with added sugar.

Although mainly used to encase a rice ball, or to form the outer layer of sushi, nori can be used as a valuable condiment. Take a sheet of nori and lightly toast it over a flame on both sides. If you do not have a gas stove the same result can be achieved with a candle. Using a pair of sharp scissors cut the sheet into quarters, and further cut each quarter into fine slithers. Sprinkle the equivalent of a quarter of a sheet of nori onto your food. It is wise to prepare only enough strips for your meal as nori does not retain its dry crisp texture, even in an airtight jar. However, it can easily be rejuvenated with some light toasting over a flame.

As an alternative to shredded strips of nori, buy a shaker of nori flakes. These bright-green, fine flakes taste slightly bitter. A sprinkling of between an eighth and a quarter of a teaspoon over your cooked cereal grains is adequate. One of the unusual benefits of nori is the small amount of vitamin C contained in the vegetable. Nori grows close to the sunlight, and the drying process during harvesting traps and preserves the vitamin C.

dips and dressings

I love the variety of colors and tastes that are used in Zen cookery. The following dips and dressings are easy to prepare, lack any preservatives or chemicals, and can provide simple yet practical ways to complete a meal. All the ingredients are available in good whole foods stores and some speciality Japanese food shops.

dashi

Ichiban Dashi is the basic stock which is fundamental to almost every soup or dip. The dashi can be stored in a jug in the refrigerator and will keep for several days.

1 quart cold water
3- inch piece of kombu
1 oz dried bonito flakes

Place the kombu in the water in a pan and bring it towards a boil. Remove the kombu just before the water boils. Continue to heat the water until it boils and then shock it with a quarter cup of cold water to bring the temperature down. Stir in the bonito flakes and bring the dashi to a boil for exactly ten seconds. Strain the dashi through a fine metal sieve and store for future use.

tempura dip no.1

As the British put salt and vinegar on their battered fish and chips, or the Germans accompany fatty cheese or sausage with sauerkraut, the Japanese use daikon and ginger in dipping sauce to help emulsify fats and oils. This dip is served cold and is ideal with deep-fried tofu and vegetables.

1 cup dashi
1 tablespoon of mirin
3 tablespoons soy sauce
2 teaspoons grated raw ginger root
¼ cup grated raw daikon

Combine the dashi, the mirin, and the soy sauce in a small steel pot and bring gently to a boil for exactly fifteen seconds. Cool and serve at room temperature. Serve with two separate small dishes containing the grated ginger and the grated daikon so guests can add the amount they wish to the dipping sauce.

tempura dip no. 2

This dip has the additional yin quality of sake which makes it better as a dipping sauce for deep-fried fish or seafood.

- 1 cup dashi
- 1 teaspoon sake
- 1 tablespoon of soy sauce
- 2 tablespoons mirin

Combine the dashi, sake, soy sauce, and mirin in a small stainless steel pan and gently heat them up. Bring the combination almost to the boil, turn off the heat and allow it to cool. This dip is good accompanied by small wedges of fresh lemon served in a separate dish.

sweet and sour salad dressing

½ cup dashi

2 tablespoons of mirin

¼ cup brown rice vinegar

½ teaspoon soy sauce

Place all the ingredients in a small stainless steel pan and bring to the boil. Let the combination simmer for 30 seconds before removing it from the flame and allowing it to cool down. This dressing mellows very pleasantly overnight in the refrigerator.

sweet
salad dressing

3 tablespoons of sake
½ cup of sesame seeds
2 tablespoons of soy sauce

Gently heat the sake in a small stainless steel pan until the aroma is strong. Take the pan away from the heat and quickly burn off the fumes of the sake with a match. While you let the sake cool, wash, then lightly roast the sesame seeds in a small cast-iron skillet until they are golden.

Using a suribachi (Japanese mortar), gently grind the sesame seeds together with the sake and soy sauce to a paste consistency. Add to any salad—it is especially good with mangetout, diced carrots, sprouts, or fresh peas.

tangy
salad dressing

4 tablespoons olive or toasted sesame oil
1 tablespoon of freshly squeezed orange juice
1 umeboshi plum or 1 teaspoon umeboshi paste
1 teaspoon finely chopped scallions

Place the oil in a bowl. Add the orange juice and either the umeboshi paste or the flesh of an umeboshi plum that has been finely sliced. Mix the ingredients very well before adding the scallions. Let the dressing sit for twenty minutes.

garnishes

the art of mukimono

In ancient Japan, food was served on simple, rustic, unglazed pottery. With time, the plate was made more attractive by covering it with a leaf and then cutting various designs around its edge. The art evolved and by the Tokugawa era, mukimono had become a fine art, and is still considered a valuable part of any chef's training.

Cutting and preparing beautiful garnishes from fruits and vegetables can display the chef's concentration and precision but wiith practice it is not hard to achieve. The following examples are a relatively easy way to begin this fascinating art.

All you will need are two good knives: a broad-bladed vegetable knife (nakiri-bocho), which is also your essential cutting utensil and a good paring knife, with a blade of two to three inches, made of high carbon-forged stainless steel.

scallion brush This can be used as a central feature for any salad, or as a garnish with a meat dish. Remove the roots of a washed scallion and cut a clean three-inch section of the stem. With the sharp tip of your paring knife, cut as many slices along nine-tenths of the scallion's length, turning it a little in the process. Finally dip the frayed section of the scallion into a bowl of iced water and this will open it up creating a brush effect.

turnip chrysanthemum This can be an impressive central feature for any large display of food, such as a buffet, or as a central feature on the table. Cut the top and root off a large turnip and, with a paring knife, peel the turnip. Use the large vegetable knife (nakiri-bocho) to cut parallel vertical slices approximately one eighth of an inch apart across the entire breadth of the turnip, but not quite down to the base. Repeat the process at right angles to your first cuts, again almost down to the base.

A useful trick here to prevent you from accidentally cutting through the entire turnip is to place two wooden chopsticks on the chopping board parallel to each other and on either side of the turnip. When you cut downwards with the knife, you can safely hit the chopsticks and still retain a good quarter of an inch of uncut turnip at the base. Make a solution of saline water (eight ounces of water and one tablespoon of sea salt) and soak the turnip for ten minutes. This will help it to "flower." As an alternative, you can soak the turnip in a solution of vegetable dye—yellow or orange. Place the finished garnish on one or two leaves picked from a shrub in your garden.

radish mushrooms A handful of delicately carved radishes can delightfully set off any bowl of green salad. Thoroughly wash six fresh radishes and remove their tap roots and stems. With a sharp paring knife, cut into the radish approximately a quarter of an inch deep all the way round the middle of the radish. To create the stem of the radish start from the top end (where the leaves were) and make short cuts to meet with the middle line that you have already formed.

radish buds You will need a handful of small, fresh radishes. Give them a good scrub and with a sharp paring knife cut the leaves and the tap root away. Place the broader section of the prepared radish on your chopping board with what was the root section pointing upwards. Make two slight gashes on four sides of the radish. For further effect, you can make a cross of two gashes in the very top (where the root tip used to be). Then simply soak the radishes in ice cold water until they open like buds.

carrot curls Take a large, fresh carrot and remove the skin with a vegetable peeler or scraper. Cut the carrot into two three-inch sections. Holding a section vertically on the chopping board, cut it into slices an inch thick with your vegetable knife.

With your paring knife make a one-inch slit in the middle of each slice—I begin by cutting the two ends with the tip of the paring knife and then simply slice the two one-inch lengths to remove the center.

It is vital that you soak the pieces in a saline solution *(see page 243),* as it makes the slices become more flexible and capable of curling. Here's the fun part: once the slices are flexible enough, poke one end of the slice through the central cut and pull it gently to form a twist.

cucumber chain Cut a four-inch section from a fresh cucumber and remove the center with a paring knife. With a sharp vegetable knife, cut the cucumber into quarter-inch rings. With the paring knife cut alternate rings, interlocking with other rings. Rejoin the cut rings by sticking their ends together, to form a chain.

cucumber twists Take a fresh cucumber and cut it into two-inch sections. With the base of one of these sections held firmly on your cutting board, slice down vertically on both sides of the cucumber to form a slice a quarter of an inch thick.

Place these two sections of the cucumber with the broad (interior) on the chopping board and cut a half inch vertical section out of each piece. You are now left with a piece of cucumber approximately two inches long by one-half inch wide that is backed by the green skin of the cucumber.

Make two vertical cuts on the wedge each beginning at either end and leaving approximately a quarter inch on each cut. Finally, simply twist the two outer sections to cross over each other to form a twist.

chapter 6

chewing well

meditation: There is an old Zen saying, "How you do anything is how you do everything."

When you rush through meals, you are likely to rush through life. —Dean Ornish

"The Japanese word kami (chew) means God or Divine Spirit. Chewing in the original Japanese meaning is to develop ourselves, to reach to the Universal Spirit." —Michio Kushi

The art of cooking naturally begins with our selection of ingredients for a meal and matching them with our condition and level of activity. The cuisine we choose, our cutting techniques, and the presentation and garnishes are all important factors in bringing together the right meal. However, all of this effort can go to waste if we do not appreciate and absorb the meal to its fullest. This process of appreciation really begins with the act of chewing.

be still

Chewing can be one of the simplest yet most profound forms of meditation that we can practice. With concentration chewing can provide us with the same time, stillness, and opportunities for self-reflection that other forms of meditation provide.

Like meditation, chewing gives us the opportunity to learn and absorb, as well as to eliminate or let go of what we do not need. Chewing forms a vital part of the spectrum of meditation that we can incorporate into our daily lives. Frequently we hear individuals say that when they wish to reflect on something they are going to "mull it over."

Chewing needs to be done slowly and with concentration. Ideally, take small mouthfuls of food and chew them until they become liquid. I recommend at first chewing for a minimum of thirty times and then slowly increasing to fifty chews per mouthful. If you are unwell, have difficulty concentrating at present or have a major decision to take, then try chewing up to one hundred times per mouthful. Even your liquid intake, especially if it is either cold or at room temperature, needs to be charged by the chi of your mouth and saliva. Instead of gulping down liquid, including water, try swilling it around in your mouth five to ten times per mouthful before you swallow. At least try to bring the liquid to the same temperature as your body. Ice cold liquid will hit the stomach hard and the stress, especially on an empty stomach, far outweighs the benefit.

Our style of chewing is conditioned in us at a very early age. As with so many facets of our lives, we learn it firsthand from our parents. Were meal times busy and chaotic? Did members of the family eat quickly or in separate rooms or at different times? Some of us had to learn at an early age to chew quickly otherwise there would be no opportunity for a second helping. At other times, we had to bolt our food because our parents tended to be late preparing breakfast or a meal before we had to go out. Some of us may have eaten in fear or anxiety as our parents argued during the meal. On the positive side, meal times could have been a relaxing and happy occasion for you. If your parents chewed their food well and appreciated it, or, better still, if your grandma sat quietly chewing every morsel, then this wisdom would have rubbed off on you as well.

Imagine you are in the woods and you need to build a campfire. You have a newspaper, a box of matches, an axe, and a small log of wood. Think of the log of wood as a representation of your meal. Imagine the little success you would achieve if you set fire to the newspaper placed underneath the log and waited for it to burst into flames. All you will be left with is the charred remains of the newspaper and a slightly scorched log. On the other hand, imagine patiently chopping the log into smaller pieces and taking one quarter of the log and shredding it into fine strips to form kindling. The finer you break down the material, the easier it becomes to light. So it is with chewing. The more you break down the food, the easier it becomes to absorb and, ultimately, the more you will benefit from the energy of the food.

the benefits of chewing

relaxation

It is possible to argue that simply sitting still for forty-five minutes every day, whether meditating or not, would leave you relaxed. With today's hectic lifestyle, any form of relaxation has to be of benefit. Rather than adopting a new program of relaxation, why not include something that you do every day anyway and, as it were, make a meal of it? All of us chew, just give it the time and concentration that it deserves.

Eating when you are relaxed also helps the digestive process. The muscles in the abdomen (the hara) are relaxed when we sit, whereas they become taut if we are standing or walking. Rushing a meal will leave us feeling tense. Eating while standing up and talking simultaneously will leave your digestive system in a state of stress, but worst of all is eating while you are walking. If the nature of your work involves you having to eat at your desk, make sure that you can shut down your computer and turn away from your work while you eat. Ideally, take yourself off to another room or sit in a park and chew your meal slowly. Hyperactive individuals tend to be those who eat in a hurry, chew very little, eat at their desks, and consequently have difficulty unwinding and relaxing. Generally, if we eat in a hurry, we work in a hurry, and the results of our efforts or creativity can match this as they become superficial, erratic, or incomplete.

satisfaction

One of the greatest pleasures that you can when you chew your food well, is feeling satisfied after a meal. You will also be pleasantly surprised to discover that you can actually eat less and still feel satisfied. Before practicing Zen cookery and learning how to chew food well, my only notion of satisfaction was to feel completely full. To leave the table feeling like I could not eat another morsel was my idea of heaven and complete satisfaction. Many people in the West struggle with their weight and consequently put themselves on strict dietary regimes. However, the matter is not simply what you eat, but how you chew and digest it.

Whole cooked cereal grains, grain by-products such as bread and pasta, and beans and vegetables, all taste more delicious as you chew. Grains, for example, become increasingly sweet as they begin to be broken down by saliva. Conversely, the longer you chew meat or gristle, the less tasty they are. However, it is within their real depth that their essence, taste and satisfaction can be revealed—within the bones, the marrow. I spent six years working and traveling, mainly third-world countries, and I was always amazed at how elderly people's faces lit up at the prospect of cracking open a bone or simply enjoying the flavor of a soup that was based on bone and marrow.

Chewing really means "making a meal of it." In other words, we integrate and appreciate every aspect of the chewing process. Our sense of awareness concerning tastes and textures can become enhanced, and the subtle flavors have the opportunity to be released and appreciated.

improved memory

Chewing well is the first step in assimilating and absorbing the nutrients from our food. Chewing well allows us to take on board ideas and information with ease and a sense of proportion. If we absorb information well in the first place we will remember it and be able to recall it easily. However, there are several layers to our memory, and it is the first three layers that can be charged, improved, and with time, easily accessed.

mechanical memory The first level of memory I call "mechanical." This is where we have the capacity to easily recall facts, details, names, telephone numbers, places, and even the time. If we chew well our chi is clear and bright. We know exactly what we are doing and can even determine a fairly accurate sense of time without resorting to a watch. This mechanical memory fluctuates according to our health, which in turn is determined by how well we have been eating and absorbing our food. When our chi is scattered, we become forgetful and begin to lose a sense of time. Within a few days of chewing well, you should notice a big improvement with this aspect of your memory.

biological memory The second level of memory I call "biological." Every cell in our body is motivated on a deep level by biological memory. This cellular memory drives every aspect of our physical being, including the function of our digestive system, circulatory system, and nervous system. Why is it that we never mechanically have to remind our lungs to breathe, or our heart to pump, or our kidneys to filter our blood? Deep down, this cellular memory has the capacity to be sharp and alert, or dulled and inefficient. In many ways, degenerative diseases could be called forms of cellular amnesia. Simply speaking, the cells and the organs that they fuel have forgotten how to perform. Chewing well is the platform on which any self-help recovery program needs to begin.

Chewing well can also activate the memory that we all hold inside of ourselves of what works for us. Taking time to chew well will spark that deep memory that perhaps you need more sleep, exercise, or recreation, or that you need to improve your communication with others. This biologically based self-reflection process can best be accessed through improved memory which is stimulated by the more you chew. As far as our health is concerned, the answers frequently lie within us rather than in the advice of others.

spiritual memory

spiritual memory The third kind of memory I call "spiritual" memory or knowing who we are and where we are in relation to our journey. This spiritual memory provides us with the profound reassurance that we are in the right place at the right time. It is the feeling of being at home wherever we are and knowing that we are on the right path. We may have had flashes or moments of this experience in our childhood which may have diminished as we began to take up academic studies. With meditation, especially our concentration through chewing, these glimpses of spiritual memory can occur more frequently and last longer. What occurs for me during these experiences is a realization that I am totally at one with my environment, a feeling that stems from a deep memory rather than the realization of a future dream. From the age of seventeen, when I began my voyage around the world, it was the deep spiritual memory of who I am that kept away any fears or anxiety. Wherever I was, I felt at home, and to this day I have no fear of the future.

stronger digestive system

The whole digestive process begins in the mouth. Naturally, the longer you chew, the more you predigest your food and the less work or strain you give to the remaining portion of your digestive system. As omnivores, it is technically easy for us to assimilate both animal and vegetable foods.

Our digestive system also has an efficient alkaline and acid balance. Saliva in the mouth is alkaline; the stomach strongly acidic; the duodenum, which acts in cooperation with the liver, gall bladder, and pancreas, is more alkaline; the small intestine is acidic; and finally the colon or large intestine is alkaline.

All carbohydrates, which traditionally formed the mainstay of the human diet, begin to be broken down by saliva. If you bolt your bread, pasta, or grain products, it will sit uncomfortably in your stomach and intestines for several hours afterwards. Conversely, tearing into pieces of meat and letting the strong acids in the stomach work on them immediately helps their absorption. Furthermore, they are absorbed more slowly in the small intestine and the colon. Animal food basically rots and putrefies in our digestive system before it is broken down further by acid in the small intestine.

To take the strain off this process, our forebears understood the importance of hanging meat and game prior to cooking and eating it. The hanging process allows the flesh, muscles, and gristle to break down and putrefy in the air before we eat it. There is a lot of sense in this approach as the food is being "predigested", before you eat it. It makes the meat easier to absorb.

Born and raised in Kenya, I have vivid memories of the markets. The meat was hung unrefrigerated, dark in color and invariably covered in flies. Years later, I was somewhat surprised to see fresh meat in a shop in England—it was bright red. I presumed that it had been slaughtered only minutes earlier, but found out that it was several days old and had been "cured" to prevent it from putrefying. Inevitably, the removal of this preliminary rotting process puts a greater strain on our digestive system, though it conforms with our culture of cleanliness and hygiene begun by the nineteenth-century, French scientist Louis Pasteur when he discovered the existence of bacteria and germs.

eliminating digestive embarrassments

Taking the time to chew your food really well can also prevent a common affliction in the West—bad breath. A small proportion of these problems emanate from stagnation in the lungs due to incapacity, lack of exercise, or smoking, but most bad breath is rooted in the stomach. Rather than neutralizing the problem with antacids, simply master the benefits of chewing very, very well and eating only when relaxed.

Another major source of digestive embarrassment can be flatulence. Again, its root cause can be traced back to a lack of proper chewing. It is not just a case of what you are eating, but how you are eating. Most flatulence is caused by the poor emulsifying of fats and oils in the digestive system. This process occurs in the duodenum (alkaline) where digestive enzymes and bile feed in from the liver, the gall bladder, and the pancreas. If we do not chew well enough and, worse still, if we fail to be relax when we eat, these helpful digestive enzymes tend to reduce their valuable input. For example, if you eat fatty, oily food in a great hurry while standing up and talking, or walking, the gall bladder will not send enough bile to emulsify the fats and oils.

The outcome is poorly digested fats entering the small and large intestine, resulting in bowel flatulence. Overall, our digestive system is our body's main interface with the outside world. Like the lungs, the gut is the only other system that has direct access to the outside world. Does that sound peculiar? Although the lungs are regarded as internal organs that never see the light of day they are, through the mouth and nostrils, "open" to the outside world. Similarly, the digestive system, all the way from the mouth to the anus is "open" to the environment through the food and liquid that we take in. A comical way of appreciating this point of view would be to imagine yourself turned inside out, with the contents of your entire gut appearing on the surface. From this perspective it is easy to see why the lungs and the gut, while being lodged deep within your system, are actually interfacing directly with the outside world. This is completely different from the internalized systems of the lymph, circulatory, and nervous systems.

stronger teeth

While the constitution of our teeth remains the product of our genes and our nutrition in childhood, the condition of our teeth remains solely our responsibility. The better you chew, the more activity you give your teeth and this, in turn, strengthens their roots and the surrounding gums. Chronic root and gum problems are largely caused by stagnant chi and stagnant blood supporting the roots and gums.

Proper chewing is a workout for the teeth and keeps them in good shape. Many of the modern convenience foods that are available in supermarkets require little chewing. Foods that are high in refined carbohydrates, such as sugar and white flour products, almost melt in your mouth.

Our ancestors understood and appreciated the yin/yang qualities of foods and realized that it was the tough yang qualities that gave us our minerals and many aspects of our constitutional strength. The yang qualities that we have learned to dismiss in recent generations include the skin, gristle, muscle, and bones of fish and animal; the skins of root vegetables; the tap roots of root vegetables; the leafy greens of root vegetables and the stalks and stems of leafy greens. Where previous generations enjoyed the tops of vegetables, kept the skin on their carrots, prized the bones and skins of fish and meat, the current generation prefers the softer and richer qualities of these foods. These include peeled and skinned vegetables; fresh salads; fruit without the skins; turkey and chicken breasts; prime cuts of beef, lamb and pork and refined (white) flour products instead of wholemeal breads and products.

The net result is that our teeth have less to chew and have consequently, become weaker. On my travels through Africa in the 1970s I was in awe of people's healthy, gleaming white, strong, and straight teeth. After all, in the ruthless process of evolution only the strongest have survived and the gateway to that survival was being able to eat. If we make the comparison between our teeth and our brain, and regard them both as a form of muscle, then what they both need is continuous use and practice for their future strength, dependability, and development.

Personally, I am eternally grateful to my African ayah (nanny), who from my earliest memory would take me on a walk to the end of our garden immediately after breakfast each day and strip a fresh twig off a bush, out of sight of my mother, and show me how to scrub my teeth and gums vigorously.

I have made it a rule to, give every tooth of mine a chance, and when I eat to chew every bite 32 times. To this rule I owe much of my success in my life.

—William Gladstone

stronger immune system

Our T-cell lymphocytes form the front line of our immune system, especially in dealing with bacteria, viruses, and parasites. Most scientific researchers agree that the thymus gland stimulates the production of these T-cells, and the more of them we have, the stronger our immune system is. The stimulus that the thymus needs to create T-cells comes from the parotid glands (located at the corner of our jaws, just behind our ears) which produce the hormone parotin.

This is where the importance of chewing comes in. Chewing stimulates the parotid glands which produce not only parotin but also saliva rich in digestive enzymes. So the more you chew, the more saliva and parotin you will produce. Effectively this not only strengthens your digestive system but also boosts your immune system.

more patience

Chewing well and slowly brings a whole new rhythm to your life and perception. By slowly absorbing not only the food you eat but also the information you receive, you are given a more grounded and rounded perspective. Rather than hurrying to conclusions or making snap decisions, it can enable you to make clear, well-reasoned responses. Ultimately it provides us with a valuable asset—patience. When we eat in a hurry and are distracted at the same time—whether by reading, talking, walking, or standing—the process puts more strain on the liver and gall bladder. Both these organs play a vital role in the digestive process and when they are balanced, traditional Chinese medicine teaches us that they provide us with tolerance and patience. On the other hand, a liver or gall bladder imbalance can make us irritable, impatient, and hypersensitive to our immediate environment. The expression "liverish" in the English language speaks of an individual who is irritable and impatient. Furthermore, when these organs are out of balance it is extremely difficult to "be in the moment." Being in the moment is probably the most valuable skill to understand and master regarding any form of Zen. Whether in meditation or cooking, it requires absolute concentration. However, with the gall bladder or liver working overtime, it is easy to fall into thinking about and planning for the future. It is also hard to relax with this kind of imbalance.

If you find yourself increasingly intolerant of others, hypersensitive to certain smells, noises, and draughts, and difficult to "be in the moment," then it is definitely worth the effort to chew slowly and well, and improve the circulation of your chi to your liver and gall bladder.

sharper intuition

A Zen approach to your cooking, combined with concentration while you are chewing, will inevitably result in sharper intuition. The essential difference between instinct and intuition is that instinct has a strong biological basis, whereas intuition is based on us aligning our chi clearly and directly. All of us have the possibility to develop intuition, and we all use it on a day-to-day basis. The problem with intuition is that its clarity will fluctuate, and this fluctuation is largely due to our current condition. The secret to sensing chi energy clearly is to be empty ourselves. If we have overeaten, been too busy, or have rushed our meal, our own chi can become chaotic. Chewing very well and peacefully is undoubtedly one of the simplest ways to "be in the moment."

Our intuition, like our brain, is a muscle that will develop the more you use it and trust it. How many times do we have a sense of what we would like to cook or eat, but then allow our logical mind to suggest something different? The "gut" feeling that we have initially is the one that we need to test, utilize, and believe more frequently if we wish to develop our intuitive side. We are all quite capable of doing this. Indeed, we have been operating from an intuitive perspective most of our lives. When we meet someone for the first time, enter a new building, or even select vegetables in the market, our initial response is the intuitive one. By spending a more time and effort on our chewing, we can access this important sense more consistently in our daily lives.

story

Between 1981 and 1991, I gave half-hour dietary consultations, back-to-back, for a five-hour period twice a week. I would use these sessions to advise patients about their diet and lifestyle. During the first few minutes of the consultation I relied on my intuition. Did I sense they were yin or yang? What kind of health imbalances did I think they might have? I would then evaluate them more mechanically, using Asian diagnosis to confirm or question my initial intuition. Finally, to help the patient find a balanced lifestyle, I would offer dietary advice and lifestyle suggestions to follow for a month

The night before the consultations, I ate simply and went to bed reasonably early. My colleagues used to think that seeing ten patients back-to-back without a break was too demanding. Several of my students acted as assistants by sitting in on the consultations to gain insights from the process. Frequently when patients booked their appointments they asked to have an earlier appointment, as they imagined I would be tired and exhausted at the end of the five hours. It could not have been further from the truth.

By the end of the five hours my concentration, perception, and intuition were far sharper than they were at the beginning. Oblivious to any hunger or thirst, my eagerness and curiosity was with the patient. Within moments of meeting a new patient, I could sense their imbalance, and I had to restrain my intuitive responses and patiently become more mechanistic in explaining and even justifying my recommendations.

All of us have had this experience with a creative project we have undertaken. The more enthusiastic, excited, and hungry we are, the clearer our judgement and perceptions are.

No matter how much or how little food you choose to consume before, during, or after work, simply make the effort to chew it really well and allow this extra charge of chi to supply your cells, your blood, and ultimately your nervous system and your intuition.

extra energy, stamina, and endurance

Zen monks in Japan were capable of incredible feats of stamina and endurance while maintaining themselves on a simple diet with limited fluid that was chewed and savored to the last drop. These tests of endurance have been traditional in Japan for centuries. Modern, nutritional sports theory is shifting away from a diet that is high in steak and eggs for athletes to one that is based on cereals and pastas; it is the slow burning of properly chewed carbohydrates that can give us the stamina. The calorific intake of a diet high in grain and legumes can be almost half that of a diet centered on meat, eggs, potatoes, and dairy foods. While the high-calorie diet can induce great spurts of powerful energy, it is difficult to maintain stamina over a long time.

During the past twenty-five years I have fasted several times for a ten-day period purely on well-cooked, slightly salted brown rice, together with simple Japanese twig tea and spring water. Far from feeling tired or hypoglycaemic, I found new levels of energy and enthusiasm. The secret to having stamina on such a simple diet is in the chewing itself. At the most I ate three bowls of brown rice a day, and I would chew each mouthful between eighty and one hundred and twenty times. Just one bowl would take forty-five minutes to complete. The first day or two, while you adjust, you may feel a little tired, irritable, and unenthusiastic. However, from day three on you will feel like you can take on the world, because you feel so well, so clear, and so intuitive.

story

In 1986 and 1987 I led survival courses in Wales, primarily for my students who were studying Asian medicine and diagnosis, and macrobiotic cooking. All the students had one thing in common—a commitment to help other people rediscover their health and intuition. I felt that the one thing missing in their education was personal experience with a chronic health problem. Far from wishing to afflict them with a serious illness, I thought a course that challenged their beliefs, and their endurance in a safe environment might provide a similar experience. Hence the idea of a survival course.

The first course I coled with an American colleague, Ron Kotsch. Older and more experienced than I was in leading these courses, Ron was a trained Outward Bound instructor. During the 1960s he had also been one of Michio Kushi's first students, and he had spent many years living with the Kushis in Brookline, Massachusetts, while he studied for his PhD in comparative religions at Harvard. Part of our course involved the twelve participants taking part in a two-day hike through the Black Mountains of Wales with only minimal equipment for shelter and six handfuls of cooked brown rice each. Far from being exhausted by the ordeal, they were all exhilarated and said they had never felt so much energy in their lives before. On their return to base camp, Ron and I completed the expedition by sending them out on a half marathon culminating in a delicious feast and some Guinness to unwind.

Around the campfire one night, Ron regaled us with a wonderful story from his days when he lived at the Kushis' home. In many ways Ron was the all-American college athlete. He was strong athletic, and keen on any sport. He would frequently shun meditation in favor of going for a jog. It seems that Michio Kushi would frequently joke at Ron's insatiable desire to jog every morning. Finally, Ron challenged him to join him one morning for a jog around the local reservoir before breakfast.

To his surprise, Michio agreed and the next morning at 7AM he appeared in a pair of 1940s black Japanese shorts, a T-shirt, and some old canvas tennis shoes. Meanwhile, Ron was there in his full jogging kit with perfect running shoes, stretching his hamstrings.

They ran round the reservoir. When they finished the lap, Michio, unmoved by the experience, and with no sign of breathlessness or perspiration inquired, "What do we do next?" Ron, panting and a fine shade of puce, suggested they go round again.

"Oh no," said Michio, "I'm going back for breakfast if this is what jogging is all about."

final note
about careful
chewing

More than two
thousand individuals die each year
in the United States from choking on their
food. It sounds unbelievable, but it is true. And,
according to the U.S. National Safety Council,
choking is among the top five causes of accidental
deaths in the United States. Since choking is a form
of asphyxiation caused by a blockage in the gullet
when someone swallows a large, unmanageable
piece of food, the risks of this occurring when you
chew well are zero. It is a sad statistic, which is
indicative of our modern era and our
tendency to eat quickly, talk when we are
eating, and not tc concentrate
on our food.

exercises

Time is such a vital factor in our lives that taking on a new discipline, such as a new meditation, can simply add further stress. However, we all need to eat and prepare food, so why not make these daily routines meditations? The following ideas are based on both common sense and Zen practice. If possible, try to integrate any or all of these practices into your mealtime over a thirty-day period and notice the difference they make in your life.

While we may all seek more freedom in our lives, it is important to consider the other side of the coin—discipline. Everyone I have met who has discovered freedom regarding their health, relationships, work, or spiritual development, have one thing in common—they worked at it. Discipline does not necessarily mean rigidity but the simple practice, on a daily basis, of cultivating what we call freedom. For example, people who have been successful in business work at it on a daily basis. They are fastidious about the mechanical side of their operation, whether it is their bookkeeping, or long-range planning, or sales operations. In relationships these people are good communicators and are constantly reassessing and reaffirming their relationship with others. As far as health and spiritual awareness is concerned, part of the discipline involves concentration, and one of the most profound expressions of this is chewing.

changing gears

Relaxing and recharging ourselves are yin activities. It is important to change our chi to become more receptive before eating. Our day-to-day work, travel, business meetings, and even the preparation of a meal, are relatively more yang activities. Whether you have just prepared a delicious meal or come in straight from work ready to eat, here are some ideas to quickly adapt your chi:

take a shower: Water can swiftly neutralize or change your chi. Whether you take a shower or simply wash your hands and face—especially with cold water—it will help to neutralize and discharge the yang chi that you may have absorbed during the day.

change the scene: If you have prepared the meal yourself and are ready to eat, it is well worth taking a few minutes to separate yourself from the kitchen and the cooking process, which itself is "yangizing," and unwind for a few moments elsewhere. A quick wash, a change of clothing, or a stretch in the garden can all help you change your chi in preparation for eating.

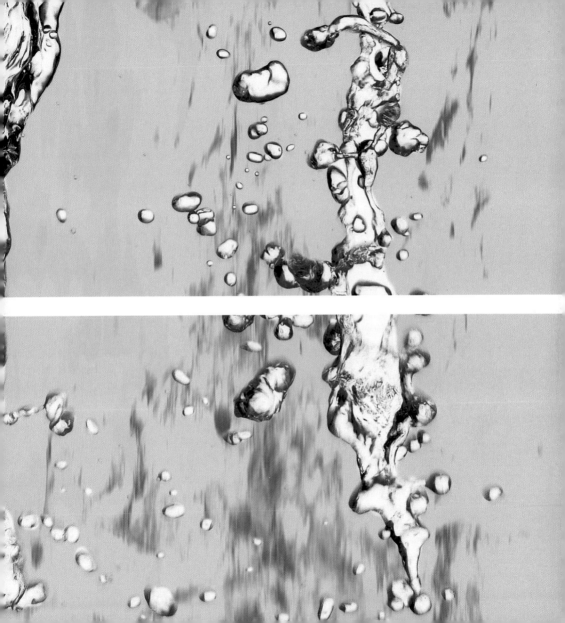

dō-in

The word "Do" (pronounced "dough") in Japanese is similar to the Chinese expression Tao, meaning the Way or Path. "In" translates as "with yourself" or "at home." Dō-in exercises have been practiced for several thousand years and include body stretches which stimulate the meridians of chi that feed our internal organs. Do-ɪn can also include the use of pressure points; rubbing or pounding the skin to stimulate the chi; and a variety of postures, breathing practices, and meditations. I learned the system in 1977 and to this day I find it the quickest and simplest way of changing my chi. Here are a few do-in exercises that can relax you prior to a meal and also stimulate your digestive system.

preparation

Wearing loose, comfortable clothing, stand with your feet parallel, approximately the same width apart as your hips. Relax your shoulders and allow your breathing to come from your belly (your hara is located about one inch below you navel).

1 Bring the palms of your hands together in a prayer posture in front of your face and rub them together vigorously. Clap loudly twice and then shake them hard to your sides, exhaling at the same time. Stretch your hands high above your head with palms facing towards the ceiling or sky. With loose wrists, shake your hands, imagining that you are polishing or dusting. Repeat this exercise three times.

2 With loose wrists, rub up and down your cheeks with the palms of your hands. Do this rubbing as you breathe out, relax, and then stop the process while you breathe in. Repeat three times.

3 Rotate your jaw clockwise in large circles three times. Repeat this counter-clockwise. Now try moving your jaw forwards and backwards three times.

4 Meridians of chi energy relating to the digestive system flow through the shoulder region. They affect the large intestine, small intestine, and gall bladder. When your shoulders feel tight it is important to relax them before eating.

Gently cradle your right elbow in the palm of your left hand and make a fist of your right hand, and keep your wrist loose. Reach across your chest with the clenched fist of your right hand and pound your left shoulder as you breathe out. Try to pound in a large circular motion incorporating the whole of the left shoulder. Repeat this exercise on your right shoulder in the same way, using your left hand.

5 You may already know that a useful technique for releasing a tight bolt or undoing a tight lid on a jar is a simple yin/yang process. The lid or bolt will be easier to release by tightening it a little before attempting to release it. The same principle holds true of this next exercise.

As you breathe in, clench your fists, wrists, forearms, shoulders, neck, jaw, and even screw up your face to tighten every muscle and sinew. Hold this position for several seconds—it is even more effective if you are quivering with the tension. Then release as you exhale sharply. Repeat the process three more times and notice how much more relaxed your shoulders have become.

6 Your hara is the physical center of your body and, of course, is the seat of your digestive system. Standing erect with your arms loose by your sides, allow your breathing to center on this region and your mind to focus on this point. Gently place both palms of your hands over this point and rotate slowly with no real pressure in a clockwise direction for two minutes.

7 Stand with your feet further apart, clench your fists, keep your wrists loose, and, as you hinge from the hips with loose knees, pound (as you breathe out) from your hips, down the sides of your legs to your ankles. Take a breath in and as you breathe out, pound on the insides of your legs from above the ankle bone up behind the shin bone to the knees and along the inside of the thighs towards the groin. Repeat this exercise three times. It stimulates the gall bladder meridian (located on the outside of the legs descending from the buttocks to the ankle) and its partner, the liver meridian (located on the inside of the legs from above the ankle through the calf and along the thigh).

8 Finish the exercise by raising one foot off the ground and shaking it vigorously from side to side. If you have space, kick this foot forward, then sideways, and then behind you like a mule kick. Repeat the exercise with the other leg.

proper breathing

Be aware of your breathing while you are chewing and enjoying your food. Take a few moments before you begin eating to allow your breath to settle lower in your abdomen in the region of the hara. If you have been rushing around, you may find that your breathing is more shallow and that there is a fair amount of movement in your shoulders and upper chest. Just sit quietly for a few moments and allow your breathing to settle in the belly, and you will notice the hara moving forwards and backwards. Avoid taking deep breaths to force this change as it may cause you to hyperventilate.

posture

Lying on the floor, standing up, or slouching on the sofa while you are eating will not help your digestive system or encourage you to chew with any concentration. Ideally, your back needs to be straight and your feet firmly on the floor with your knees one fist apart. The easiest way to make sure that your back is straight is to stretch your arms high above your head, bend your head back to look at the ceiling, look forward and then, while maintaining this posture, return your elbows to your sides and place your palms in your lap.

You may prefer to sit Japanese style—sei-za (pronounced say-tsar). Obviously you will need a low table for this posture and if you are not used to it, it can be uncomfortable. Begin by kneeling on the floor with your back straight and the upper part of your feet resting on the floor. Your knees should be one fist apart, your big toes touching, and your heels facing outwards. Gently sit down so that your buttocks are cradled between your heels and the inside edges of your feet. As with the sitting position previously mentioned, you can stretch your spine and return your palms to your lap.

mudra

This hand posture is the most powerful technique that I have learned to aid chewing. I have noticed that my chewing becomes stronger and far more concentrated when I practice this. You will also notice that the thumbs and forefinger are united in the mudra. The lung meridian ends at the thumb and the large intestine meridian begins on the forefinger. In Chinese medicine, these meridians are partners and are associated with absorption and elimination.

Bring your palms together as if in prayer posture in front of you. Curl your little finger, ring finger, and middle finger so that they overlap on to the back of the opposite hand. Keep the forefingers touching each other and the thumbs touching each other. Between taking mouthfuls, place your utensil on the table, make this mudra and place your hands between your thighs and knees with your forefingers pointing towards the floor ahead of you. The best experiment you can make is to try chewing a mouthful thirty times without using the mudra, and then try thirty times while practicing this mudra. You will be amazed at how more effective and powerful your chewing becomes.

chopsticks or a fork?

I prefer to use wooden chopsticks when I am concentrating on my chewing. They are fairly easy to master and prevent you from eating too quickly or putting too much food into your mouth. I also like the texture and feel of wood in my mouth compared to steel or silver. It is a personal choice, but if you have not tried wooden sticks I can highly recommend them to add discipline, focus, and concentration to your chewing.

liquids and meals

Since the majority of vegetables, soups, stews, and noodles are made up of liquid anyway, your increased power of chewing is going to liquefy them further. Naturally it is important to drink when you are thirsty, but preferable to drink after the meal rather than during or before it. If the liquid is cold, make sure that you swill it around your mouth several times to bring it up to body temperature before you swallow it. Soup is an important part of a meal, as it soothes and prepares the digestive system for the yang or heavier part of the meal to follow. Sometimes I like to end my meal with a soup. It is entirely your choice.

light exercise

Rather than lie on the sofa after a meal, try taking a short stroll, which aids the digestive process. Walking is the easiest exercise as it involves using the muscles of the abdomen which stimulate the hara and the intestinal region.

eating before sleeping

The old adage of "breakfast like a king, lunch like prince, and sup like a pauper" makes tremendous sense. Our digestive system does not enjoy a heavy workload straight before bed. Ideally, avoid eating for at least two hours before you go to sleep. Digestion continues for up to two hours after you eat, and while you are still awake or active this process is quicker and more efficient. Going to sleep directly after a meal puts more strain on your liver, gall bladder, and small intestine, often causing you to wake the next morning feeling tired, unmotivated and even irritable.

The liver and gall bladder, in particular, recharge themselves between the hours of 1AM and 5AM, and if you have eaten just before going to bed you are not going to give these organs the rest that they need. Also, while you are asleep other digestive organs—the pancreas, colon, stomach, and small intestine—are having to work overtime to cope with the late supper.

The late night snack that I have found the easiest to digest is soba noodles and broth. Follow the recipe in Chapter Three but leave out the tempura.

chapter 7

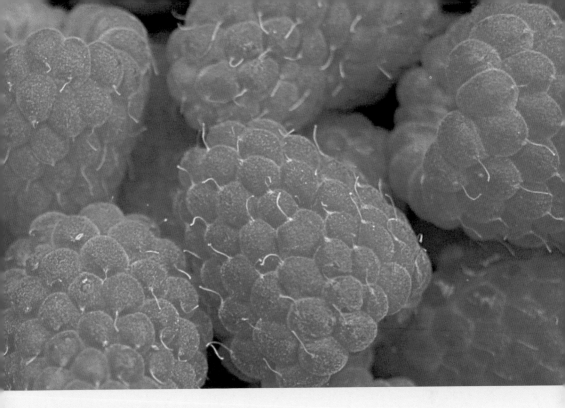

conclusion

meditation: If you cannot find the truth right where you are,

where else do you expect to find it? —Dogen

One of the points on the Eight Fold Path of Zen is "right understanding," meaning we should develop our powers of awareness and judgement to their fullest.

By adopting the Zen approach to cooking, we will have a broader perspective on the benefits of food and the way it can be cooked, as well as being aware of its impact on our creativity and self-expression. Every food source on this planet is available to us, and we have enormous choice over how we prepare our food, whether or not we chew it well, and whether or not we present it gracefully.

greater

awareness in cooking

Cooking is an area of our lives in which we can exercise considerable freedom and can realize our individual potentials by making the most of the many varieties, colors, tastes, and ingredients available. With such a huge range of possibilities before us, we need to have "right understanding" to discover which ingredients and cooking styles may best suit our lifestyles and conditions at any given time.

With a true understanding of the ideas and principles of Zen cooking outlined in this book, it is possible to take any ingredient and prepare it in any number of different ways. Real freedom with food involves taking what is local and appropriate to your environment and preparing it simply according to your needs. For example, if you have no desire to experiment with brown rice, tofu, sea vegetables, or exotic Japanese seasonings, it is quite appropriate to continue using familiar ingredients and cooking styles but to adapt their preparation. You may decide to experiment with new garnishes and presentations, as well as simply to look out for fresher, better quality ingredients.

the seven stages

Our consciousness—even on a primitive level—has been developing from the very moment that we were conceived. Our awareness as human beings develops through a series of seven stages as we grow, and each of these stages plays a vital role in our understanding of the world around us. There are no rights or wrongs about these stages of awareness, simply that they evolve, one after the other, as we develop physically, and that we have the choice of operating from any of these stages at any time.

# of awareness

While these seven stages correlate with the development of our consciousness, they are equally valuable in understanding the stages through which we proceed in our search for the truth of freedom—what Buddhists call satori, Hindus nirvana, or Christians "a state of grace." Parallel to these stages of our consciousness and spirituality are the levels on which we value our food and cooking. While reading through these seven stages, make a note of which stage or stages you operate from in relation to food and cooking.

① mechanical stage

All human life begins at this stage where, even as a small cluster of cells, the human embryo develops a mechanical, reactive awareness. This phase continues throughout our lives and enables us to adapt automatically and spontaneously to any given situation. Our cells adapt, our breathing can alter, our pulse rates can increase—all on a mechanical reactive level.

In terms of food and cooking the mechanical stage relates to impulsive, spontaneous, and automatic action. I am hungry, therefore I eat. No real thought goes into what is being eaten or how it is prepared—the hunger and desire to eat is simply fulfilled by food. Thousands and thousands of individuals operate on this level every day without giving any real attention to what they eat.

sensory awareness

Our senses develop at an early stage in the embryo and form our most important level of consciousness when we are born. It is on this level of awareness that we develop our sense of smell, touch, hearing, taste, and sight. Of all these senses, newborn infants have a heightened sense of smell, enabling them to locate and find their mothers' breasts. Senses of touch, taste, hearing, and sight develop slightly later. At this level, it is possible to be aware of comfort, beauty, and desire.

As far as food is concerned, this sensory level is satisfied by food that tastes and smells delicious. A primitive level of smell is one that still exists deep into adulthood. How easy it is to remember someone entering your kitchen and exclaiming "that smells delicious!" It is often the first comment that a guest may make at the table, rather than commenting on the texture or the taste. When we operate from this level of awareness, we have great appreciation for the sensory quality of food. However, if we are stuck on this level we are only attracted to food that brings us a deep sense of comfort based on taste, texture, smell, and presentation. To develop a clear understanding of this sensory level of awareness, try cooking for children—especially someone else's!

sentimental or emotional awareness

At a fairly young age, we all begin to develop this quality of judgement. It is at this stage that we show our approval of food. We have begun to discover what we like and dislike and can express this opinion clearly. As our awareness grows and develops through the sensory stage, we can begin to perceive what we like and dislike. We can distinguish hot and cold, wet and dry, light and darkness.

As adults it is easy to revert to this emotional or sentimental level of awareness concerning our food. It shows especially when discerning quite strongly what we like or dislike. Since this level of awareness is deeply rooted in our early development, we can have strong sentimental associations with foods that our mother prepared. It is on this sentimental level that we value foods that remind us of our childhood. Whether it was our mother's cooking or old-fashioned creamy "nursery" foods, you may notice how attached you are to these types of foods in your own cooking.

4

conceptual awareness

It is at this level of development that we begin our search for the truth. As children we bombard our parents and teachers with questions. This is the world of ideas, theories, and debate, and includes such questions as "Why is the sky blue?" We develop this level of conceptual awareness in our adulthood, adding muscle to our intellect. It is the world of rationalizing, of discovering causes and effects, and a continued search for the truth. Modern science and technology have evolved from this level of awareness.

In terms of food, it is our concern about modern nutritional theories. Here we speculate whether a meal has adequate minerals, protein or carbohydrates, and we can begin to lose sight of our intuition while we hold onto the truth of scientific data. Our great-grandparents never heard of vitamins—although they used them—nor did they use the term "calorie." When we operate on this level, we tend to see food as a complex quantity of chemicals that need to be balanced rationally. Modern cook books, recipes, and even teaching styles come less from the experience and wisdom of our mothers and grandmothers and more from the teachings of domestic science. If we are more concerned about the specific nutrient value of our foods rather than how it tastes or appears, then we are operating more on this level of awareness.

social awareness

As children, we begin to develop a curiosity for the world beyond ourselves and our family around the age of three. Suddenly there is a whole new world beyond our front door. We develop an appetite for meeting others, and we form views about the world beyond our immediate families. Seeds for social awareness are sown at school and at home. The focus is on gaining an understanding of morals and ethics. This is the foundation for our discovery of what is right and wrong, of what is acceptable behavior, and for acquiring a concern for what is fair for all of humanity.

More and more individuals are beginning to spread their social awareness into the area of food and its origins. Consumers are now questioning the origin of their food, its quality, and whether it has been subject to chemical and hormone treatments. The issue of genetically modified foods (GMF) is currently of great social concern, as are certain farming methods because of their long-term detrimental impact on the soil.

"You must be
the change you

wish to see in
the world."

—Mahatma Gandhi

6

ideological awareness

The social and ideological stages of awareness form the platform for a deeper search for freedom and justice. As children, this level of awareness is sparked by our families' religious or spiritual practices. Whether or not there is much encouragement in this domain, children will constantly ask the big questions—"Where do we come from?" or "Who is God?" It is on this level that we begin to practice philosophy or religion and to incorporate different spiritual practices into our daily lives.

In our relationship with food, this level is associated with preparing and eating foods either on religious grounds or from our own personal ideology. Whether one is Sikh, Muslim, Hindu, Christian, Buddhist, or Jain, there are always guidelines or precepts concerning the choice and preparation of food. Individuals can also make a choice simply from a personal ideological point of view. Vegetarianism is a clear-cut example of this. However, deciding that you will no longer eat meat because it no longer tastes good would be operating more from the sensory level of awareness.

supreme awareness

This is the goal of every major religion in the world—to find peace within yourself and express unconditional love and gratitude. In essence, it is our quest to discover true freedom. Whether we call this the Christian state of grace or the Buddhist satori, it means discovering individual freedom. It is easy to imagine that this select group of individuals may be limited to ascetic monks living in a monastery or a cave in their twilight years, completely "at one" with themselves and the universe. I believe that people who have attained this level of awareness are extremely playful and operate on all the preceding six levels of awareness with equal ease and flexibility.

True freedom about food would mean being happy with meager amounts, being satisfied easily, appreciating yet not being limited by the sensory quality of food, enjoying what is prepared with love, and understanding the truth about food through continued chewing and self-reflection. These are all natural building blocks toward creating a new sense of freedom that we can all enjoy in our relationship with food.

final thoughts

Our future freedom as a species lies in our own hands. From a pessimistic standpoint the future looks pretty dim: high levels of pollution, overpopulation, global warming, soil erosion, deforestation, and the growing risk of degenerative disease due to overconsumption. Our towns and cities, which developed out of fortified communities designed to protect us from other tribes, have turned their back on nature and virtually imprisoned their inhabitants.

The first step in creating a future for us all lies in embracing, honoring, and appreciating the natural world that we inhabit. How can we connect more strongly with it? Should we all move to the country and downsize our working environment to live in isolated cottages and small communities across the land?

These are pretty unrealistic solutions and there is a much simpler approach. The easiest way to absorb the natural world in which we live is through our relationship with food. Choosing good quality, natural foods that maintain their integrity—their wholeness—is a start. The natural world provides us with the nutrients to enrich the land from which we draw our food, and the preparation and consumption of this food fuels our blood which in turn supports our nervous system and our consciousness. It is the easiest, yet the most profound path that any of us can take to gain greater clarity, adaptability, and freedom. Chew very well!

Designer: Simon Balley
Editor: Alison Moss
Text Editor: Malcolm Day

Sourcebooks, Inc.
P.O. Box 4410, Naperville, Illinois 60567-4410

TEL: (630) 961-3900
FAX: (630) 961-2168

Printed and bound in Italy by Amadeus
MQ 10 9 8 7 6 5 4 3 2 1

ISBN: 1-57071-615-3

dedication
For my children: Justin, James, Chloe, Josh, Luke, Chiara, Alma

Photo Credits
Neil Sutherland: pp 2-3, 119, 153, 179, 233
Lucy Mason: pp 20-21, 48, 55, 82-83, 98-99, 140-141, 156-157, 194-195, 219, 268-269
Peter Aprahamian: pp 22, 46, 76, 96, 162, 196, 248
Sue Wilson: pp 25, 26, 53, 302
Chris Alack: pp 34-35, 43, 79, 100, 112-113, 115, 127, 130, 142, 208, 216-217, 241, 252, 258, 274, 278, 297
Chris Tubbs: pp 86, 124, 144, 270